THE
READY RESOURCE FOR

*Relief Society*

TEACHINGS OF PRESIDENTS
OF THE CHURCH

**GORDON B. HINCKLEY**

# THE
# READY RESOURCE FOR

# *Relief Society*

## TEACHINGS OF PRESIDENTS
## OF THE CHURCH
## GORDON B. HINCKLEY

# TRINA BOICE

CFI
AN IMPRINT OF CEDAR FORT, INC.
SPRINGVILLE, UTAH

This is not an official publication of The Church of Jesus Christ of Latter-day Saints. The opinions and views expressed herein belong solely to the authors and do not necessarily represent the opinions or views of Cedar Fort, Inc. Permission for the use of sources, graphics, and photos is also solely the responsibility of the authors.

ISBN 13: 978-1-4621-1962-2

Published by CFI, an imprint of Cedar Fort, Inc.
2373 W. 700 S., Springville, UT 84663
Distributed by Cedar Fort, Inc., www.cedarfort.com

Library of Congress Cataloging-in-Publication Data

Names: Boice, Trina, 1963- author.
Title: The ready resource for Relief Society : teachings of presidents of the
   Church. Gordon B. Hinckley / Trina Boice.
Other titles: Gordon B. Hinckley
Description: Springville, Utah : CFI, an imprint of Cedar Fort, Inc., [2016]
   | Includes bibliographical references and index.
Identifiers: LCCN 2016046217 (print) | LCCN 2016048612 (ebook) | ISBN
   9781462119622 (perfect bound : alk. paper) | ISBN 9781462127337 (epub,
   pdf, mobi)
Subjects: LCSH: Hinckley, Gordon Bitner, 1910-2008--Teachings. | Church of
   Jesus Christ of Latter-day Saints--Doctrines--Study and teaching. | Relief
   Society (Church of Jesus Christ of Latter-day Saints)
Classification: LCC BX8609 .B65 2016 (print) | LCC BX8609 (ebook) | DDC
   230/.9332--dc23
LC record available at https://lccn.loc.gov/2016046217

Cover design by Shawnda T. Craig
Cover design © 2016 by Cedar Fort, Inc.
Edited and typeset by Rebecca Bird

Printed in the United States of America

10 9 8 7 6 5 4 3 2 1

Printed on acid-free paper

This book is dedicated to my two sisters, Tera Duncan and Tracey Long, who have always been valiant examples to me of faithful women and mothers. Thank you for truly living the gospel with joy and gladness, for your missionary service, and for raising amazing families who bless the lives of so many!

# Other Books by Trina Boice

*Base Hits and Home Run Relationships:*
*What Women Wish Guys Knew*

*My Future's So Bright, I Gotta Wear Shades:*
*An LDS Teen's Guide to Success*

*Dad's Night: Fantastic Family Nights*
*in 5 Minutes or Less*

*The Ready Resource for Relief Society:*
*Teachings of Presidents of the Church* (8 volumes)

*Sabbath Solutions: More Than 350 Ways*
*You Can Worship on the Lord's Day*

*Easy Enrichment Ideas:*
*Thinking Outside the Green Gelatin Box*

*Climbing Family Trees: Whispers in the Leaves*

*Bright Ideas for Young Women Leaders*

*Great Ideas for Primary Activity Days*

*Exciting Ideas for Ward Activities: Parties with a Purpose*

*Primarily for Cub Scouts*

*How to Stay UP in a DOWN Economy*

*You're What?: 103 Creative Ways to*
*Announce Your Pregnancy*

*The Gift of Love: A Visual Pun Book of the Heart*

# Contents

# CONTENTS

# *Acknowledgments*

I want to thank Cedar Fort for inviting me to share this annual book series adventure with them! I also want to send a big thank you to my editor, Rebecca Bird, for all of her help with this edition.

A special thanks goes to my wonderfully supportive family for taking care of everything around me while I was busy pounding away at my computer keyboard. My husband and four sons inspire me to try harder and be better every day. I'm also forever grateful for my extended family's continued enthusiastic support, unconditional love, and kind encouragement.

Thank you to all the faithful members of the Church who valiantly magnify their callings and give of their time and talents to bless those around them. Heavenly Father knows that when we teach others, we learn more deeply ourselves. They say that God loves all people, but especially teachers, because they remind Him of His son!

Not only should we read the scriptures and have a meaningful gospel study plan, but we should *feast* on the scriptures—we have been commanded to! It is my hope that this book serves as a helpful utensil with which for you to enjoy your meal!

# Introduction

President Gordon B. Hinckley served as the fifteenth President of the Church of Jesus Christ of Latter-day Saints for thirteen years. The teachings in the 2017 Relief Society and Priesthood course manual come from President Hinckley's sermons and articles as he served in the Church. He had a wonderful sense of humor and a positive outlook on life. It hasn't been that long since he passed on to the other side of the veil, so most of the Relief Society sisters will remember him fondly. You will enjoy helping the sisters in your ward get to know this man of God better, as well as have a desire to joyfully live the gospel.

*The Ready Resource for Relief Society* for 2017 is designed to be a helpful, inspiring resource to make lesson preparation easier and more exciting. You can find the new Church manual for Relief Society and priesthood lessons at: www.lds.org/manual/teachings -of-presidents-of-the-church-gordon-b-hinckley.

The gospel means "the good news" and should bring us great joy! Members of the Church of Jesus Christ of Latter-day Saints should be the happiest people around! May you feel the Savior's loving arms enfold you as you teach your dear sisters and feed His sheep!

Each chapter includes

- Hymns appropriate for the lesson
- Quick summaries of the lesson material
- Quotes to supplement your class discussions
- Suggested artwork to display during your presentation
- Recommended videos to show during class
- Object lessons to add pizzazz and encourage student participation
- Related articles for further research
- Weekly challenges to encourage your sisters to immediately apply what they learned during your lesson

- Space to take personal notes and record inspiration as you prepare your thoughts
- Handouts that can be copied, printed, and given to the sisters

Two other teaching tools that will strengthen spiritual growth and family relationships are the seminary doctrinal mastery passages (perfect for parents of teens) and correlating topics in the Church's missionary manual, *Preach My Gospel: A Guide to Missionary Service* (perfect for parents of future and current missionaries). Remember: You're not teaching lessons—you're teaching sisters!

A suggested handout is also provided. Each set of handouts equals the same size as half a sheet of paper, so copying is quick and easy.

The most important tool is the Holy Ghost, which will help you know how to tailor each lesson to meet the needs of your sisters. Pray for the Holy Ghost to guide your study preparation before your lesson and to provide inspiration during your lesson. As you live the commandments and do your utmost to magnify your calling, you will receive personal revelation and direction on how you should share the lessons with your sisters.

The best lessons are not lectures, but rather, discussions where everyone participates. Try to involve the sisters and encourage them to share their experiences and testimonies of the principles you are teaching. They should leave your class feeling edified, enriched, and excited to live the gospel with joy!

Integrating various learning styles into your lessons improves retention and attention, assists in lesson planning, and inspires participants. Everyone learns differently, so be sure to include a variety of teaching techniques. Try using some of the following ideas during your lessons.

## STUDENT-CENTERED

- Assignments
- Debates
- Brainstorming
- Field trips
- Case studies
- Games
- Discussions
- Panels
- Instructional games
- Questions
- Memorizing
- Class journals
- Note-taking
- Open-ended stories
- Oral readings
- Songs

- Role-playing
- Crafts
- Testimonies
- Worksheets

## TEACHER-CENTERED

- Jokes and puns
- Demonstrations
- Lectures
- Surveys
- Oral readings
- Catchphrases and taglines
- Storytelling
- Questions
- Summaries
- Personal emails
- Guest speakers
- Dramatization
- Personal photos and videos
- Feedback

## MATERIALS-CENTERED

- Bulletin board
- Social media
- Chalkboard
- Handouts
- Charts and maps
- Quizzes and tests
- Displays
- eBooks
- Flash cards
- Mobile apps
- Flannel board
- Graphs
- DVDs
- Original films
- Flip charts
- Overhead transparencies
- Comics
- Pictures and artwork
- PowerPoint presentations
- Posters
- Whiteboard
- Puppet shows
- Treasure hunts
- Dramatization
- Sound recordings

## CHRIST-CENTERED

- Testimonies
- Spiritual guidance
- Prayers
- Temple attendance
- Scriptures
- Devotionals
- Service projects
- Church standards
- Building faith
- Unconditional love
- Artwork

MUSIC: Music has the potential to effectively teach and invite the Spirit—better than almost any other teaching technique. Included with each lesson are song suggestions that the class could sing or simply learn from by reading the lyrics. Inviting others in your ward to provide special musical numbers during your lessons can bind hearts together and uplift everyone. You can find the LDS hymnbook online, where you can download songs, listen to them online, and do searches by topics, titles, and even scriptures! (Visit www.lds.org/churchmusic.)

You can also use songs from seminary, Young Women, and Primary, as well as music that has been published in Church magazines. Also on the Church's website are learning materials on topics such as conducting music, understanding symbols and terms, and finding great ideas to add variety to singing.

Check out these great resources:

- Church Hymns on iTunes: itunes.apple.com/us/app /lds-hymns/id332640791?mt=8
- "Free Ward Choir Music," arr. Linda Pratt: www .freewardchoirmusic.com/
- Free LDS sheet music: www.soundsmithmusic.com/

QUOTES: Quotes from Church authorities can be used to inspire the mind and uplift the heart. It's nice to have some quotes written on the board at the front of the room for students to read before class starts. It helps set the tone and gets them thinking about the topic. Some of the suggested handouts in this book use such quotes, but you can also design your own handouts with your favorite quotes. You can do a search on www.lds.org with a keyword about the topic you're searching for. More quotes can be found online at

- www.quotegarden.com
- www.thinkexist.com
- www.inspirational-quotes.info
- www.brainyquote.com
- www.quotationspage.com
- www.wisdomquotes.com

ART: Beautiful artwork can teach in a way that words alone cannot, especially for visual learners. Your church building's library may have some larger prints of older pictures that are numbered. Those numbers will be different than the ones found on pictures in the *Gospel Art Book*. Picture suggestions in this book will only include references to the *Gospel Art Book*.

# INTRODUCTION

You can purchase a *Gospel Art Book* from distribution centers or from www.ldscatalog.com. The book is spiral-bound and contains 137 color pictures as well as a useful index that connects each image to the scriptures. They are organized into the following six categories:

- Old Testament
- New Testament
- Book of Mormon
- Church History
- Gospel in Action
- Latter-day Prophets

You can access many pictures on the Church's website at www .lds.org/media-library/images. There you can also find cool memes (inspirational picture quotes), desktop wallpapers to let your sisters know about, and the ever-popular Mormonads.

The pictures online are organized into almost every category you can imagine. The site now allows you to create images, as well as share your own photos and videos! Get in the habit of checking the Church's website often because there are always new features being added.

Some terrific Church resources that provide excellent artwork on gospel themes can also be found at:

- LDS Photos: www.lds.org/media-library/images
- BYU Religious Education Image Archive: www.lib.byu.edu /collections/religious-education-image-archive/
- Joseph Smith: Prophet of God (maps, artwork, photos, documents, and more!): www.josephsmith.net
- Bible Photographs: www.lds.org/scriptures/bible-photos
- Church History Photographs: www.lds.org/scriptures/history -photos
- Temples: www.lds.org/church/temples/find-a-temple

VIDEOS: The Church has some excellent videos that can be found online and downloaded to your computer. Most church buildings have Wi-Fi, which will allow you to stream Church videos, rather than download them to your computer. If you choose to stream media, be sure to practice in your building before your lesson to ensure everything works correctly. To display the videos, you'll need either a TV or a projector (as well as a white wall or screen) in order to share them with your class. You will also want to bring your own cords and adaptors to connect your laptop to the equipment. Find out ahead of time what equipment your library has so you can properly prepare.

# INTRODUCTION

There is a fantastic series of videos available online called *The Life of Jesus Christ Bible Videos*. You can find them at www.lds.org/bible-videos, where new ones are continually being added. There you can also download a free mobile app for viewing the videos on your phone.

YouTube hosts several "channels" of videos officially released by the Church as well at

- www.youtube.com/user/MormonMessages
- www.youtube.com/user/LDSPublicAffairs

Most church buildings block YouTube on their Wi-Fi, so plan ahead by downloading any YouTube Church videos that you want to share during class. You'll also find a lot of other great LDS videos on YouTube that were uploaded by members of the Church. Many chapels have Internet access, but again, be sure to do a test run with your equipment before you decide to include videos in your lesson. Your lessons shouldn't be entertainment-focused, but spirit-focused.

OBJECT LESSONS: Object lessons capture the students' interest and increase understanding by teaching the concepts in a unique way. The Savior often used physical objects that were familiar to His listeners to illustrate simple principles. Each lesson offers ideas for object lessons that could be an effective introduction to the topic or a fun way to keep the class engaged.

ARTICLES: It is such a blessing to read from Church leaders each month in the various Church magazines. Teach your class how to find material they can share with their families during family home evening lessons or to help them prepare Sacrament talks in the future. Each lesson in this book includes only a few suggested articles, but there are so many more! One of the biggest blessings of preparing your lessons each month will be the focused time you get to spend researching specific gospel topics. You will learn so much more than you'll ever have time to share with your sisters in class on Sunday! Teaching Relief Society is a wonderful excuse to truly immerse yourself in gospel study. Enjoy it!

CHALLENGES: A meaningful addition to each lesson is the use of a personal challenge that can be extended to the sisters at the end class. Perhaps it should be called an "invitation for application." The sisters need to *apply* what they've learned after they leave your classroom. If they don't *use* the lesson material to improve their lives and strengthen their testimonies, then they aren't growing spiritually from your efforts. You can offer the suggested challenge, one of your own, or invite the class to choose their own personal goal that will allow them to delve deeper and stretch further. In the end, we won't be judged by all of the religious trivia we can recite to the Lord at the judgment seat, but by the Christlike qualities we have acquired. The Lord cares much more about who we are becoming than He does about what we are doing.

DOCTRINAL MASTERY PASSAGES: Previously referred to as seminary scripture mastery passages, the Church has officially changed them to be called "doctrinal mastery passages." Parents of seminary students may want to learn some of the same one hundred scripture passages that their teens are learning. Learning these verses can strengthen their home and family. Teachers can mention which verses correlate with each lesson's topic. What a terrific tool it is to commit scriptures to memory together. You can see all of the seminary manuals and resources at www.lds.org/manual/seminary.

PREACH MY GOSPEL: The Church is currently experiencing a wonderful wave of new missionaries as the Lord hastens His work. To help the sisters in your ward become more familiar with this guide to missionary service, consider including topical passages from *Preach My Gospel* and talking about how to share the lesson with nonmember friends. A digital version of the manual can be found at www.lds.org /manual/preach-my-gospel-a-guide-to-missionary-service.

As a Relief Society teacher, take time to read chapter 10 of *Preach My Gospel*. Pages 175 to 194 offer insights in how to improve your teaching skills.

ADDITIONAL RESOURCES: Visit the section of the Church's website that is dedicated to Relief Society resources. This section can be found under the "Serve and Teach" menu tab on the home page at www.lds.org. When you click on "Resources," you will discover all kinds of fantastic tools to help you in your sacred calling! Then, click on "Leadership Training Library" to see even more helpful tools.

The steps suggested for how to prepare a lesson include

- Use approved lesson materials
- Seek the guidance of the Spirit
- Study your lesson in advance
- Consider the needs of your sisters
- Organize the lesson
- Seek the gift of teaching

Be sure to read about the life of Gordon B. Hinckley in the front of the 2017 Relief Society handbook and share your testimony of this great prophet. The sisters will enjoy seeing pictures of him and getting to know and love him through your lessons this year.

*TEACHING IN THE SAVIOR'S WAY*: A wonderful manual has been created to help instructors use the same teaching techniques that the Savior used. It was designed specifically to train anyone who has a Church calling to formally teach. A digital version of this manual can be found on the Church's website at www.lds.org/manual /teaching-in-the-saviors-way.

There is also a lovely video called "Teaching the Gospel in the Savior's Way" (www.lds.org/media-library/video/2012-06-003-teaching -the-gospel-in-the-saviors-way?lang=eng&_r=1) that encourages teachers to facilitate engaging discussions, rather than give lectures. We teach more like the Savior taught when we

- Prepare to teach
- Help the class discover the gospel
- Invite the class to act
- Provide students the opportunity to teach
- Love our students

Jesus was the master teacher. He still is! He cared deeply about each person He taught. In His lessons, He used variety, honesty, symbolism, and storytelling. He also challenged His listeners to make specific changes in their lives. The more you study and teach the gospel, the greater your own understanding will be.

Use the scriptures each time you teach, and encourage your class to feast from their pages. As you come to love the scriptures, your class will feel that passion and be inspired to feast upon them as well. Your task as a teacher is to invite your sisters to "come unto Christ." In order to do that effectively, you must create an atmosphere where the Holy Ghost will be welcome and be able to testify to the hearts of your students.

You give voice to the gospel principles taught each week, but it is the testifying power of the Holy Ghost that touches hearts and transforms lives. May you feel the Spirit guide and direct you as you do your best to magnify this calling!

Articles about teaching with the Spirit:

- Henry B. Eyring, "Rise to Your Call," *Ensign*, November 2002.

- William D. Oswald, "Gospel Teaching—Our Most Important Calling," *Ensign*, November 2008.
- Dallin H. Oaks, "Gospel Teaching," *Ensign*, November 1999.
- Bruce R. McConkie, "The Teacher's Divine Commission," *Ensign*, April 1979.
- David M. McConkie, "Gospel Learning and Teaching," *Ensign*, November 2010.

Videos about teaching with the Spirit:

- "Seek Learning by Faith": www.lds.org/service /teaching-the-gospel/principles-and-methods-of-teaching /teach-by-the-spirit
- "Prepare and Teach by the Spirit": www.lds.org/media-library /video/2015-12-3000-prepare-and-teach-by-the-spirit
- "Testimony of Truth": www.lds.org/media-library/video/2012 -11-9225-testimony-of-truth?category=doctrine-and-covenants /section-40-section-84
- "Welcome: Annual Auxiliary Training: Relief Society": www .lds.org/media-library/video/auxiliary-training-videos/2014 -auxiliary-training
- "If We Teach by the Spirit": www.lds.org/media-library/video /2010-07-142-if-we-teach-by-the-spirit

*Chapter One*

# THE RESTORATION OF THE GOSPEL—THE DAWNING OF A BRIGHTER DAY

. . . . . . . . . . . . . . . . . . . . . . . . . . . . . . . . . . . . .

## MUSIC

"The Sacred Grove," *Children's Songbook*, 87.
"High on the Mountain Top," *Hymns*, no. 5.
"Joseph Smith's First Prayer," *Hymns*, no. 26.
"The Day Dawn is Breaking," *Hymns*, no. 52.
"The Glorious Gospel Light Has Shone," *Hymns*, no. 283.
"A Key Was Turned in Latter Days," *Hymns*, no. 310.

. . . . . . . . . . . . . . . . . . . . . . . . . . . . . . . . . . . . .

## SUMMARY

After the Savior ascended into heaven, His Church and its ordinances and teachings lost their purity. Priesthood authority and correct doctrine were restored in 1830, when a prophet of God was again chosen. The Church of Jesus Christ of Latter-day Saints offers the fulness of the gospel to the world today—which gospel will never be destroyed.

The Book of Mormon provides us with additional scriptures that teach us the gospel and testify that the Savior lives and has established His kingdom here on earth. The priesthood has been restored so that we can participate in saving ordinances and be blessed on earth and in heaven. How wonderful it is to be a member of the Lord's Church!

. . . . . . . . . . . . . . . . . . . . . . . . . . . . . . . . . . . . .

## QUOTES

🔹 "Joseph the Prophet . . . became the means, in God's providence, to restore the old truths of the everlasting gospel of Jesus Christ, the plan of salvation, which is older than the human race. It is true, also, that his teachings were new to the people of his day because they had apostatized from the truth—but the principles of the gospel are the oldest truths in existence. They were new to Joseph's generation, as they are in part to ours, because men had gone astray, been cast adrift, shifted hither and thither by every new wind of doctrine which cunning men—so called progressives—had advanced. This made the Prophet Joseph a restorer, not a destroyer, of old truths." (*Teachings of Presidents of the Church: Joseph F. Smith* [1998], 18.)

🜲 "We declare to the world that the fulness of the gospel of Jesus Christ has been restored to the earth." (L. Tom Perry, "The Message of the Restoration," *Ensign*, May 2007.)

🜲 "The dawn of the dispensation of the fulness of times rose upon the world. All of the good, the beautiful, the divine of all previous dispensations was restored in this most remarkable season." (Gordon B. Hinckley, "The Dawning of a Brighter Day," *Ensign*, May 2004.)

🜲 "The Lord permitted these few poorly armed and ill-clad men at Valley Forge and elsewhere to defeat a great army, . . . a few against the many, but the few had on their side the Lord God of heaven, that gave them victory. With it there came political liberty and religious liberty, all in preparation for the day when a young boy would come forth and would seek and make contact with the Lord and open the doors of heaven again." (*Teachings of Spencer W. Kimball* [1982], 403.)

## ART

Daniel Interprets Nebuchadnezzar's Dream, no. 24
Missionaries: Sisters, no. 110
Service, no. 115
Kirtland Temple, no. 117
Nauvoo Illinois Temple, no. 118
Salt Lake Temple, no. 119
Young Couple Going to the Temple, no. 120
Temple Baptismal Font, no. 121
Joseph Smith, no. 122
Brigham Young, no. 123
Gordon B. Hinckley, no. 136

## VIDEOS

"The Restoration": www.lds.org/media-library/video/2008-06-01-the
-restoration

"The Apostasy and Restoration": www.lds.org/media-library/video
/2016-02-0001-the-apostasy-and-restoration

"His Sacred Name—An Easter Declaration": www.lds.org/media
-library/video/youth-curriculum/april-the-apostasy-and-the
-restoration

"Restoration of the Priesthood": www.lds.org/media-library/video
/2010-05-1130-restoration-of-the-priesthood?category=youth
-curriculum/april-the-apostasy-and-the-restoration

"The Apostasy and the Restoration—What the Restoration Means for
Me": www.lds.org/media-library/video/2012-10-004-the-apostasy
-and-the-restoration-what-the-restoration-means-for-me?category
=youth-curriculum/april-the-apostasy-and-the-restoration

## OBJECT LESSONS

- Pass out gum to the class and tell them to chew it for about five minutes to get all of the flavor out of it. Now ask the class to put it back into the wrapper and mold it into the original form. Many men have tried unsuccessfully to recreate Christ's true Church. Only with the Savior's help was Joseph Smith able to restore the Lord's Church.

- Show the class some tarnished silver spoons. Talk about the restoration of Christ's true Church while you polish the silver. Discuss how the beauty was always there, but that no one could see it until it was restored. Isn't it interesting that a silversmith is someone who is trained to restore beauty and the Prophet Joseph's surname was Smith?

- Pass out pictures that illustrate each section in this lesson. Invite the sisters to talk about each particular gospel truth and how our lives are enriched because of the correct knowledge we now have about it. The lesson will naturally become a very sweet testimony meeting.

## ARTICLES

Dieter F. Uchtdorf, "Are You Sleeping through the Restoration?,"
*Ensign*, May 2014.

L. Tom Perry, "The Message of the Restoration," *Ensign*, May 2007.

James E. Faust, "The Restoration of All Things," *Ensign*, May 2006.

Gordon B. Hinckley, "His Latter-day Kingdom Has Been Established," *Ensign*, May 1991.

Bruce R. McConkie, "The Lord God of the Restoration," *Ensign*, November 1980.

Hugh W. Pinnock, "The Gospel Restored," *Ensign*, May 1980.

Jeffrey R. Holland, "This, the Greatest of All Dispensations," *Ensign*, July 2007.

Russell M. Nelson, "'Thus Shall My Church Be Called,'" *Ensign*, May 1990.

D. Todd Christofferson, "Come to Zion," *Ensign*, November 2008.

Henry B. Eyring, "The True and Living Church," *Ensign*, May 2008.

M. Russell Ballard, "The Truth of God Shall Go Forth," *Ensign*, November 2008.

## CHALLENGE

Write down your specific testimony of each of the gospel principles that are featured in this lesson. (Gospel principles include apostasy, restoration, the First Vision, Joseph Smith, priesthood keys, the Godhead, family, and salvation for the dead.) Give examples from your life that illustrate how you learned that each principle is true.

## DOCTRINAL MASTERY PASSAGES

- Moroni 10:4–5
- Joshua 24:15
- Ezekiel 37:15–17
- Daniel 2:44
- Amos 3:7
- Matthew 16:15–19
- Ephesians 4:11–14
- 2 Thessalonians 2:1–3
- Joseph Smith—History 1:15–20
- D&C 8:2–3
- D&C 84:33–39
- D&C 121:36

## *PREACH MY GOSPEL*

1, 5–7, 31–32, 34–37, 44, 103–14

NOTES

_____

_____

_____

_____

_____

_____

_____

_____

_____

_____

_____

_____

_____

_____

_____

_____

_____

_____

_____

_____

_____

_____

_____

_____

_____

The dawn of the dispensation of the fulness of times rose upon the world. All of the good, the beautiful, the divine of all previous dispensations was restored in this most remarkable season.

Gordon B. Hinckley, "The Dawning of a Brighter Day," *Ensign*, May 2004

The dawn of the dispensation of the fulness of times rose upon the world. All of the good, the beautiful, the divine of all previous dispensations was restored in this most remarkable season.

Gordon B. Hinckley, "The Dawning of a Brighter Day," *Ensign*, May 2004

# Chapter Two

# AN ENSIGN TO THE NATIONS, A LIGHT TO THE WORLD

. . . . . . . . . . . . . . . . . . . . . . . . . . . . . . . . .

## MUSIC

"High on the Mountain Top," *Hymns*, no. 5.
"'Twas Witnessed in the Morning Sky," *Hymns*, no. 12.
"The Day Dawn Is Breaking," *Hymns*, no. 52.
"Behold! A Royal Army," *Hymns*, no. 251.
"The Glorious Gospel Light Has Shone," *Hymns*, no. 283.
"Come, All Ye Sons of God," *Hymns*, no. 322.

. . . . . . . . . . . . . . . . . . . . . . . . . . . . . . . . .

## SUMMARY

These are the last days! We have much to do to prepare the world for the Savior's Second Coming. Wickedness is increasing at an ever-rapid pace and our homes and values are being assaulted on every side. Still, the positive influence that we, as members of the Church can have, can be very powerful if we are not afraid to stand as witnesses of Christ. As witnesses, we can help the pure in heart to feel secure as we offer them an anchor against the storms howling around us all. We can prevent the adversary from having any power over our homes and hearts by obeying the Lord's commandments that have been designed to protect us. There is safety and power in following the Prince of Peace!

As we remember the "grand picture" and the "broader vision" of God's work, we will magnify our callings and truly understand that even our smallest efforts help to build the kingdom of God here on earth. What an honor it is to play a part in the divine destiny of God's work!

# CHAPTER TWO

## QUOTES

🌸 "Ancient prophets looked with enthusiastic anticipation to our dispensation when the fulness of the gospel would be restored and preached among all nations, and when final preparations would be made for the Second Coming and ultimate reign of the King of Kings, our Savior. Great eternal blessings, keys, and secrets of the gospel, which have been kept "hid from before the foundation of the world," were reserved to come forth in this final dispensation to bless our lives. How privileged we are to live in these momentous times!" (J. Lewis Taylor quoted in "I Have a Question," *Ensign,* June 1975.)

🌸 "Members of the Church need to influence more than we are influenced." (M. Russell Ballard, "The Effects of Television," *Ensign,* May 1989.)

🌸 "If we will pursue a steady course, our very example will become the most effective argument we could ever advance for the virtues of the cause with which we are associated." (Gordon B. Hinckley, "Pursue the Steady Course," *Ensign,* January 2005.)

🌸 "The Church is like a great caravan—organized, prepared, following an appointed course, with its captains of tens and captains of hundreds all in place. What does it matter if a few barking dogs snap at the heels of the weary travelers? Or that predators claim those few who fall by the way? The caravan moves on. Is there a ravine to cross, a miry mud hole to pull through, a steep grade to climb? So be it. The oxen are strong and the teamsters wise. The caravan moves on. Are there storms that rage along the way, floods that wash away the bridges, deserts to cross, and rivers to ford? Such is life in this fallen sphere. The caravan moves on. Ahead is the celestial city, the eternal Zion of our God, where all who maintain their position in the caravan shall find food and drink and rest. Thank God that the caravan moves on!" (Bruce R. McConkie, "The Caravan Moves On," *Ensign,* November 1984.)

## ART

Daniel Refusing the King's Food and Wine, no. 23
Three Men in the Fiery Furnace, no. 25
Daniel in the Lions' Den, no. 26
Calling of the Fishermen, no. 37

The Good Samaritan, no. 44
Go Ye Therefore, no. 61
Jesus Carrying a Lost Lamb, no. 64
Enos Praying, no. 72
Moroni Hides the Plates in the Hill Cumorah, no. 86
Captain Moroni Raises the Title of Liberty, no. 79
The Foundation of the Relief Society, no. 98
Family Prayer, no. 112
Service, no. 115

• • • • • • • • • • • • • • • • • • • • • • • • • • • • • • • • • • • •

## VIDEOS

"Temple Square": www.lds.org/media-library/video/missionary
/introduction-to-mormons
"The Church at a Glance": www.lds.org/media-library/video/2013-02
-1010-the-church-at-a-glance?category=missionary/introduction
-to-mormons
"What Mormons Believe": www.lds.org/media-library/video/2013-02
-1020-what-mormons-believe?category=missionary/introduction
-to-mormons
"The History of Mormonism": www.lds.org/media-library/video/2013
-02-1030-the-history-of-mormonism?category=missionary
/introduction-to-mormons
"Seek and Attain the Spiritual High Ground in Life": www.lds.org
/media-library/video/2009-03-0020-seek-and-attain-the-spiritual
-high-ground-in-life

• • • • • • • • • • • • • • • • • • • • • • • • • • • • • • • • • • • •

## OBJECT LESSONS

🌸 Invite the class to join you in an activity called "Think, Pair, Share." First, ask the sisters to *think* about what they have done in their community, school, or neighborhood to be a light and radiate the joy of living the gospel. After thirty seconds, divide the sisters into *pairs* and have them *share* their answers.

🌸 Ask everyone if they like to eat cake. Have them list the ingredients in the cake and ask if they like to eat the raw ingredients separately. Explain that eating raw cake ingredients is a lot like life; separately there are some bitter times, some raw, hurtful times, and some dry, bland times. But there are also good times! Together, God is able to blend them all together to create a life that is meaningful, useful, and enjoyable! The Lord has warned us that perilous times are coming, but that they are a part of the plan. He has asked us to stand for righteousness and to be a light to the rest of the world in dark times. Serve cupcakes to your class. Talk about the "sweetness" the gospel brings to our lives.

🔹 Print out copies of a paper that says "Yes" on one side and "No" on the other. Ask the class questions while they hold up the paper with their answer on it. Questions might include the following:
- Are you involved on a committee at your child's school?
- Do you belong to a professional organization?
- Does your neighborhood have a Neighborhood Watch group?
- Are you a member of a club?
- Do you attend meetings in your area?
- Do you know any nonmembers?
- Do you know your next-door neighbor?
- Do you ever have block parties on your street?

Then, introduce your lesson topic and continue asking questions during the lesson for the sisters to answer by holding up their papers.

## ARTICLES

Boyd K. Packer, "'The Standard of Truth Has Been Erected,'" *Ensign*, November 2003.

Joseph Anderson, "Light and Knowledge to the World," *Ensign*, November 1972.

Spencer W. Kimball, "Learn—Then Teach," *Ensign*, November 1980.

Joseph B. Wirthlin, "Let Your Light So Shine," *Ensign*, November 1978.

Thomas S. Monson, "Be an Example and a Light," *Ensign*, November 2015.

Chad Lewis, "The World Needs to See and Feel Your Light," (Brigham Young University devotional, March 25, 2014; speeches.byu.edu).

## CHALLENGE

Think of a way you could help the Lord and His Church shine brightly in your community. For example, you could serve on a school

PTA board or committee, begin a Neighborhood Watch program so neighbors can get to know each other and keep their streets safe, create an interfaith choir with other churches in your area, coordinate a "Christmas in Bethlehem" event, or invite Scouts from other wards or denominations to enjoy an activity with your ward's Scouts.

## DOCTRINAL MASTERY PASSAGES

- Mosiah 2:17
- Moses 1:39
- Moses 7:18
- Abraham 3:22–23
- Ezekiel 37:15–17
- Daniel 2:44
- Amos 3:7
- Matthew 5:14–16
- Matthew 16:15–19
- Ephesians 4:11–14
- Joseph Smith—History 1:15–20
- D&C 18:10–11, 15–16

## PREACH MY GOSPEL

1–3, 5–7, 12–13, 19–21, 31–32, 34–36, 47, 54, 71, 82, 92, 96–102, 107–8, 138–39, 155–58, 168–70, 187, 195–99

## NOTES

_____

_____

_____

_____

_____

_____

_____

_____

_____

_____

_____

_____

_____

Members of the Church need to influence more than we are influenced.

M. Russell Ballard, "The Effects of Television," Ensign, May 1989

Members of the Church need to influence more than we are influenced.

M. Russell Ballard, "The Effects of Television," Ensign, May 1989

Members of the Church need to influence more than we are influenced.

M. Russell Ballard, "The Effects of Television," Ensign, May 1989

Members of the Church need to influence more than we are influenced.

M. Russell Ballard, "The Effects of Television," Ensign, May 1989

# Chapter Three

## CULTIVATING AN ATTITUDE OF HAPPINESS AND A SPIRIT OF OPTIMISM

### MUSIC

"Happy Song," *Children's Songbook*, 264.
"Be Happy!," *Children's Songbook*, 265.
"Come, Rejoice," *Hymns*, no. 9.
"Scatter Sunshine," *Hymns*, no. 230.
"Father, Cheer Our Souls Tonight," *Hymns*, no. 231.

### SUMMARY

It is easy to become depressed and cynical when we focus on the ugly and difficult things in this world. We often feel discouraged and overwhelmed when we wake up with a gigantic list of things we need to accomplish each day. Because of the Savior's many enemies, He had every reason to feel bitter, angry, and filled with despair, yet He told us to be of good cheer! There is still beauty all around!

As members of the Church of Jesus Christ of Latter-day Saints, we know how the "story" ends and we know who wins, so we should be the happiest, most optimistic people on earth! By focusing on the good things of this world, we develop a powerful spirit of gratitude and can feel more joy in our lives each day.

### QUOTES

"One of the challenges of this mortal experience is to not allow the stresses and strains of life to get the better of us—to endure the varied seasons of life while remaining positive, even optimistic. . . . We can't predict all the struggles and storms in life, not even the ones just around the next corner, but as persons of faith and hope, we know . . . the best is yet to come." (L. Tom Perry, "Let Him Do It with Simplicity," *Ensign*, November 2008.)

🪷 "Find happiness in ordinary things, and keep your sense of humor." (Boyd K. Packer, "Do Not Fear," *Ensign*, May 2004.)

🪷 "Rather than thinking in terms of a day, we perhaps need to snatch happiness in little pieces, learning to recognize the elements of happiness and then treasuring them while they last." (James E. Faust, *Ensign*, October 2000.)

🪷 "I think it is incumbent upon us to rejoice a little more and despair a little less." (*Teachings of Presidents of the Church: Howard W. Hunter* [2015], 69.)

🪷 "Happiness does not depend on what happens outside of you, but on what happens inside of you. It is measured by the spirit with which you meet the problems of life." (Spencer W. Kimball quoted in James E. Faust, "A Vision of What We Can Be," *Ensign*, March 1996.)

## ART

The Lord Created All Things, no. 2
Ruth Gleaning in the Fields, no. 17
Christ Healing the Sick at Bethesda, no. 42
Mary and Martha, no. 45
The Ascension of Jesus, no. 62
Jesus at the Door, no. 65
Joseph Smith Seeks Wisdom in the Bible, no. 89
Elijah Appearing in the Kirtland Temple, no. 95
Joseph Smith in Liberty Jail, no. 97

## VIDEOS

"Bearing Our Burdens with Hope": www.lds.org/media-library/video /2015-04-001-bearing-our-burdens-with-hope
"My Calm in the Storm": www.lds.org/media-library/video/2013-04 -01-my-calm-in-the-storm?category=family-history/member -experiences

"Be of Good Cheer": www.lds.org/media-library/video/2014-01-018
-be-of-good-cheer

"Stay in the Boat and Hold On!": www.lds.org/media-library/video
/topics/hope

"Finding Happiness": www.lds.org/media-library/video/2009-01-59
-finding-happiness

"Be of Good Cheer": www.lds.org/media-library/video/2012-03-1110
-be-of-good-cheer

## OBJECT LESSONS

🌸 Your Relief Society can accomplish so much good for your community. Determine if there are any service project ideas the sisters could do together while they listen to your lesson. (For ideas, go to www.lds .org/church/news/21-service-projects-done-at-byu-womens-conference.)

🌸 Before your lesson, choose a sister in the ward who is new or who the others don't know very well. Secretly, find out what some of her favorite things are (cookie, flower, color). Put them in a "Happiness Basket" that you will give to her during the lesson. Tell the class about her in a short "Sister Spotlight" and then challenge her to spotlight a sister the following week. This might be a new tradition your Relief Society embraces to get to know one another better and to focus on a spirit of optimism.

🌸 Invite some Primary children to come in and sing, "If You're Happy." Talk about what things you can do to remember to be happy, and what actions you can take when you're feeling optimistic!

## ARTICLES

Anne Marie Rose, "Facing Trials with Optimism," *Ensign*, May 1996.

Marvin J. Ashton, "A Voice of Gladness," *Ensign*, May 1991.

Henry B. Eyring, "A Priceless Heritage of Hope," *Ensign*, May 2014.

Dieter F. Uchtdorf, "The Infinite Power of Hope," *Ensign*, November 2008.

Quentin L. Cook, "'Hope Ya Know, We Had a Hard Time,'" *Ensign*, November 2008.

## CHALLENGE

Surround yourself with things that make you truly happy and feel joy—whether it be flowers, delicious food, pictures of loved ones, cute decorations on your counter, or diffused essential oils. Make a list of all of your favorite things and begin incorporating them into your daily life. No need to wait for a special occasion to use those beautiful china plates your grandmother gave you!

. . . . . . . . . . . . . . . . . . . . . . . . . . . . . . . . . . . . . . .

## DOCTRINAL MASTERY PASSAGES

- 2 Nephi 2:25
- Alma 41:10
- Ether 12:6
- Ether 12:27

- Moroni 7:45
- Matthew 5:14–16
- 2 Timothy 3:16–17
- D&C 18:10, 15–16

. . . . . . . . . . . . . . . . . . . . . . . . . . . . . . . . . . . . . . .

## *PREACH MY GOSPEL*

65, 90–91, 115, 117–18, 168–69

. . . . . . . . . . . . . . . . . . . . . . . . . . . . . . . . . . . . . . .

## NOTES

_____

_____

_____

_____

_____

_____

_____

_____

_____

_____

_____

_____

FIND HAPPINESS IN ORDINARY THINGS, AND
KEEP YOUR SENSE OF HUMOR.

BOYD K. PACKER, "DO NOT FEAR," *ENSIGN*, MAY 2004

FIND HAPPINESS IN ORDINARY THINGS, AND
KEEP YOUR SENSE OF HUMOR.

BOYD K. PACKER, "DO NOT FEAR," *ENSIGN*, MAY 2004

FIND HAPPINESS IN ORDINARY THINGS, AND
KEEP YOUR SENSE OF HUMOR.

BOYD K. PACKER, "DO NOT FEAR," *ENSIGN*, MAY 2004

*Chapter Four*

# THE PIONEER HERITAGE OF FAITH AND SACRIFICE

• • • • • • • • • • • • • • • • • • • • • • • • • • • • • • • • • • •

## MUSIC

"To Be a Pioneer," *Children's Songbook*, 218.
"Whenever I Think about Pioneers," *Children's Songbook*, 222.
"Come, Come, Ye Saints," *Hymns*, no. 30.
"For the Strength of the Hills," *Hymns*, no. 35.
"They, the Builders of the Nation," *Hymns*, no. 36.
"True to the Faith," *Hymns*, no. 254.
"Carry on," *Hymns*, no. 255.

• • • • • • • • • • • • • • • • • • • • • • • • • • • • • • • • • • •

## SUMMARY

As a member of the Church of Jesus Christ of Latter-day Saints, you have inherited an inspiring legacy of faith from the Mormon pioneers. Their faith and sacrifice shows us the perfect example of transforming faith into belief and then into powerful actions that can change the world.

Sacrifice is one of the most important principles of the gospel; it is the principle upon which the Atonement is centered; it is the crowning test to determine if we will put God first in our lives. When we are willing to sacrifice our worldly riches, time, energy, talents, and personal desires, we become like Jesus Christ and are worthy to enter into our Father's presence. The more we give up what we want for God's will, the more easily His will becomes our own. Having a testimony of the gospel is not enough; we must live it.

## QUOTES

🌸 "The primary purpose of the law of sacrifice is twofold: to test us and to assist us to come unto Christ." (M. Russell Ballard, "The Law of Sacrifice," *Ensign*, October 1998.)

🌸 "The Lord isn't asking us to load up a handcart; He's asking us to fortify our faith. He isn't asking us to walk across a continent; He's asking us to walk across the street to visit our neighbor. He isn't asking us to give all of our worldly possessions to build a temple; He's asking us to give of our means and our time despite the pressures of modern living to continue to build temples and then to attend regularly the temples already built. He isn't asking us to die a martyr's death; He's asking us to live a disciple's life." (M. Russell Ballard, "The Truth of God Shall Go Forth," *Ensign*, November 2008.)

🌸 "One day beyond the veil of death, the much-praised pioneers will praise their modern counterparts." (Neal A. Maxwell quoted in "Brace for Future by Pondering the Past," *Church News* [July 30, 1988].)

## ART

Adam and Eve Kneeling at an Altar, no. 4
Abraham Taking Isaac to Be Sacrificed, no. 9
The Ten Commandments, no. 14
The Crucifixion, no. 57
Emma Smith, no. 88
Emma Crossing the Ice, no. 96
Joseph Smith in Liberty Jail, no. 97
The Foundation of the Relief Society, no. 98
Exodus from Nauvoo, February–May 1846, no. 99
Mary Fielding Smith and Joseph F. Smith Crossing the Plains, no. 101
Handcart Pioneers Approaching the Salt Lake Valley, no. 102
Nauvoo Illinois Temple, no. 118
Joseph Smith, no. 122

## VIDEOS

"Let Us Be Men": www.mormonchannel.org/watch/series/mormon
    -messages/let-us-be-men-4

"Our Pioneer Legacy": www.lds.org/media-library/video/2010-07-119
-our-pioneer-legacy

"Our Pioneer Legacy": www.lds.org/media-library/video/topics/pioneers

"Faith of our Fathers: Pioneers Then and Now": www.lds.org/media
-library/video/2012-07-11-faith-of-our-fathers-pioneers-then-and
-now?category=topics/pioneers

"President Uchtdorf Faith of Our Fathers": www.lds.org/media-library
/video/2011-07-47-president-uchtdorf-faith-of-our-fathers?category
=topics/pioneers

## OBJECT LESSONS

Give each person some peanuts to hold onto and ask them to come up with a list of things worth sacrificing for (for example: getting married in the temple, raising successful children, graduating from college, serving a mission, having a large retirement fund). Ask what specific sacrifices would need to be made in order to reach those goals. Invite those who are willing to make those sacrifices to give up one of their peanuts. It has been said that we make a sacrifice for the Lord when we give up something good for something better. Pass out a Snickers bar to those sisters who expressed a desire to make a sacrifice. Explain that those things were just "peanuts" compared to the greater blessing available to us.

Write the word "God" on a piece of paper and post it on a wall in the classroom. Post another paper with the word "Worldliness" on the opposite wall. Invite the class to stand and face the wall of their choosing. Ask, "Is it possible to face both walls at the same time?" Then read Matthew 6:24: "No man can serve two masters: for either he will hate the one, and love the other; or else he will hold to the one, and despise the other. Ye cannot serve God and mammon." Discuss the sacrifices and benefits involved in facing either wall.

## ARTICLES

Earl C. Tingey, "Prophets—Pioneer and Modern Day," *Ensign*, May 2007.

Mary Ellen Smoot, "Pioneer Shoes through the Ages," *Ensign*, November 1997.

Dallin H. Oaks, "Following the Pioneers," *Ensign*, November 1997.

M. Russell Ballard, "Faith in Every Footstep," *Ensign*, November 1996.

M. Russell Ballard, "The Blessings of Sacrifice," *Ensign*, May 1992.

Russell M. Nelson, "Roots and Branches," *Ensign*, May 2004.

## CHALLENGE

Write a list of sacrifices you can make in your life and the blessings that would come as a result. What blessings do you enjoy now because of the sacrifices made by the pioneers or by your ancestors? Write down what kind of legacy you would like to leave your descendants. Identify one thing you could do this week to begin to create a legacy of faith and sacrifice for your posterity.

## DOCTRINAL MASTERY PASSAGES

- 1 Nephi 3:7
- Ether 12:6
- Moroni 7:45
- Moses 7:18
- Abraham 3:22–23
- Joshua 24:15
- Proverbs 3:5–6
- Daniel 2:44
- Matthew 16:15–19
- Ephesians 4:11–14
- D&C 82:10

## PREACH MY GOSPEL

8, 18, 22, 31, 35–36, 38, 61, 66, 80, 88, 90–102, 115–16, 155

## NOTES

_____

_____

_____

_____

_____

_____

_____

One day beyond the veil of death, the much-praised pioneers will praise their modern counterparts.

Neal A. Maxwell quoted in "Brace for Future by Pondering the Past," Church News (July 30, 1988)

One day beyond the veil of death, the much-praised pioneers will praise their modern counterparts.

Neal A. Maxwell quoted in "Brace for Future by Pondering the Past," Church News (July 30, 1988)

One day beyond the veil of death, the much-praised pioneers will praise their modern counterparts.

Neal A. Maxwell quoted in "Brace for Future by Pondering the Past," Church News (July 30, 1988)

One day beyond the veil of death, the much-praised pioneers will praise their modern counterparts.

Neal A. Maxwell quoted in "Brace for Future by Pondering the Past," Church News (July 30, 1988)

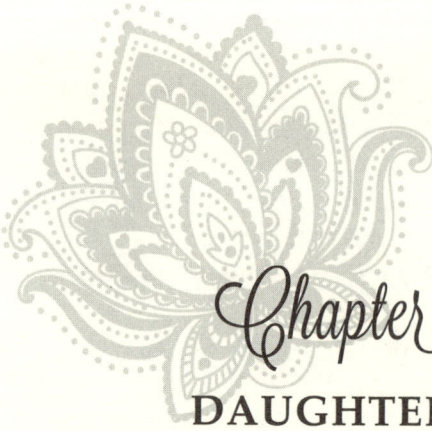

# *Chapter Five*

## DAUGHTERS OF GOD

. . . . . . . . . . . . . . . . . . . . . . . . . . . . . . . . . . .

### MUSIC

"Have I Done Any Good?," *Hymns*, no. 223.
"Improve the Shining Moments," *Hymns*, no. 226.
"Let Us All Press On," *Hymns*, no. 243.
"We Are All Enlisted," *Hymns*, no. 250.
"Put Your Shoulder to the Wheel," *Hymns*, no. 252.
"True to the Faith," *Hymns*, no. 254.

. . . . . . . . . . . . . . . . . . . . . . . . . . . . . . . . . . .

### SUMMARY

Since the very beginning, faithful women have played vital roles in the growth of the Lord's kingdom on earth. Did you know that the Relief Society is the largest women's organization? There is no limit to the good our sisters can do in the world and in the Church.

Whether we serve in the Nursery or on the General Relief Society Board, we are valued and are invited to partake of His marvelous work and wonder. Heavenly Father offers every spiritual gift and blessing He has to every valiant woman. The Lord expects women to seek for light and truth, as well as lead others to Him.

We become Christlike when we do His work. It is an honor to search for the Lord's lost lambs and to feed His sheep, because we know the Shepherd will return! Women have a natural ability to nurture, serve, and care for others—just like the Savior.

. . . . . . . . . . . . . . . . . . . . . . . . . . . . . . . . . . .

### QUOTES

✿ "In order to do our part as women under the Lord's plan, we must stand strong and immovable in *faith*, strong and immovable in *family*, and strong and immovable in *relief*. . . . My dear sisters, our prophet, whom I sustain with all my heart, has said that there is a better way than the way of the world. He has called upon the women of the Church to stand together for righteousness. He has said that if we are united and speak with one voice, our strength will be incalculable." (Julie B. Beck, "What Latter-day Saint Women Do Best: Stand Strong and Immovable," *Ensign*, November 2007; emphasis in original.)

🌸 "Much of what we accomplish in the Church is due to the selfless service of women. Whether in the Church or in the home, it is a beautiful thing to see the priesthood and the Relief Society work in perfect harmony. Such a relationship is like a well-tuned orchestra, and the resulting symphony inspires all of us." (Quentin L. Cook, "LDS Women Are Incredible!," *Ensign*, May 2011.)

🌸 "More than ever before we need women of faith, virtue, vision, and charity . . . who can hear and who will respond to the voice of the Lord." (M. Russell Ballard, "Women of Righteousness," *Ensign*, April 2002.)

🌸 "There is no other arrangement that meets the divine purposes of the Almighty. Man and woman are His creations. Their duality is His design. Their complementary relationships and functions are fundamental to His purposes. One is incomplete without the other." (Gordon B. Hinckley, "The Women in Our Lives," *Ensign*, November 2004.)

🌸 "What a different world and Church this would be if every Latter-day Saint sister excelled at making, renewing, and keeping covenants; if every sister qualified for a temple recommend and worshipped more often in temples; if every sister studied the scriptures and doctrines of Christ and knew them so well that she could teach and defend those doctrines at any time or place." (Julie B. Beck, "What Latter-day Saint Women Do Best: Stand Strong and Immovable," *Ensign*, November 2007.)

• • • • • • • • • • • • • • • • • • • • • • • • • • • • • • • • •

## ART

Adam and Eve Kneeling at an Altar, no. 4
Jesus and the Samaritan Woman, no. 36
Mary and Martha, no. 45
Mary and the Resurrected Jesus Christ, no. 59

Go Ye Therefore, no. 61
Jesus Carrying a Lost Lamb, no. 64
Jesus at the Door, no. 65
Emma Smith, no. 88
The Foundation of the Relief Society, no. 98
Mary Fielding and Joseph F. Smith Crossing the Plains, no. 101
Missionaries: Sisters, no. 110
Service, no. 115

## VIDEOS

"Daughters of God": www.lds.org/media-library/video/2012-01-015
    -daughters-of-god
"Daughters in My Kingdom: The History and Work of Relief Society":
    www.lds.org/media-library/video/2010-09-0010-julie-b-beck
"Relief Society—Daughters in My Kingdom": www.lds.org/media
    -library/video/2011-09-0020-relief-society-daughters-in-my-kingdom
"Guardians of Virtue: Young Women Song": www.lds.org/media
    -library/video/2010-12-15-guardians-of-virtue-young-women-song
"Mothers and Daughters": www.lds.org/media-library/video/2010-06
    -0070-mothers-and-daughters
"What Manner of Men and Women Ought Ye to Be?": www.lds.org
    /media-library/video/2008-11-0050-what-manner-of-men-and
    -women-ought-ye-to-be

## OBJECT LESSONS

This might be a fun Relief Society lesson to invite the young women to join. Let the sisters see each other recite the Young Women Theme and Relief Society Declaration. Have the sisters sit according to their generations (under 20, 30–40, 40–50, 60+), and have each group answer various questions according to how their age group sees the world.

Turn off all the lights and cell phones. Open the door a crack and talk about how light enters the room. Have the sisters turn on flash-lights or cell phones one at a time, representing the good acts of kindness, service, and leadership we perform. As we bring truth and light to a dark world, it becomes brighter. All of the sisters united in Relief Society can illuminate the world!

## ARTICLES

Quentin L. Cook, "LDS Women are Incredible!," *Ensign*, May 2011.

Barbara B. Smith, "Women for the Latter Day," *Ensign*, November 1979.

Silvia H. Allred, "Every Woman Needs Relief Society," *Ensign*, November 2009.

Julie B. Beck, "Fulfilling the Purpose of Relief Society," *Ensign*, November 2008.

Henry B. Eyring, "The Enduring Legacy of Relief Society," *Ensign*, November 2009.

Julie B. Beck, "The Vision of Prophets regarding Relief Society: Faith, Family, Relief," *Ensign*, May 2012.

Thomas S. Monson, "The Mighty Strength of the Relief Society," *Ensign*, November 1997.

. . . . . . . . . . . . . . . . . . . . . . . . . . . . . . . . . . . .

## CHALLENGE

Make an extra effort with the sisters you visit teach this month, whether it be an extra phone call, email, text, or home visit. Write a list of all the ways you can truly lift their burdens, give comfort, teach, enrich, and make them feel Christ's love for them.

. . . . . . . . . . . . . . . . . . . . . . . . . . . . . . . . . . . .

## DOCTRINAL MASTERY PASSAGES

- 1 Nephi 3:7
- Moroni 7:45
- Moroni 10:4–5
- Moses 1:39
- Isaiah 29:13–14
- Daniel 2:44
- Matthew 5:14–16
- Ephesians 4:11–14
- 2 Thessalonians 2:1–3
- Joseph Smith—History 1:15–20
- D&C 18:10, 15–16

. . . . . . . . . . . . . . . . . . . . . . . . . . . . . . . . . . . .

## *PREACH MY GOSPEL*

84, 87, 118

. . . . . . . . . . . . . . . . . . . . . . . . . . . . . . . . . . . .

## NOTES

_____

_____

Much of what we accomplish in the Church is due to the selfless service of women. Whether in the Church or in the home, it is a beautiful thing to see the priesthood and the Relief Society work in perfect harmony. Such a relationship is like a well-tuned orchestra, and the resulting symphony inspires all of us.

Quentin L. Cook, "LDS Women Are Incredible!," *Ensign*, May 2011

Much of what we accomplish in the Church is due to the selfless service of women. Whether in the Church or in the home, it is a beautiful thing to see the priesthood and the Relief Society work in perfect harmony. Such a relationship is like a well-tuned orchestra, and the resulting symphony inspires all of us.

Quentin L. Cook, "LDS Women Are Incredible!," *Ensign*, May 2011

# *Chapter Six*

# HOW MIGHTY A THING IS PRAYER

. . . . . . . . . . . . . . . . . . . . . . . . . . . . . . .

## MUSIC

"A Child's Prayer," *Children's Songbook*, 12.
"Joseph Smith's First Prayer," *Hymns*, no. 26.
"Did You Think to Pray?," *Hymns*, no. 140.
"Sweet Hour of Prayer," *Hymns*, no. 142.
"Prayer Is the Soul's Sincere Desire," *Hymns*, no. 145.
"Before Thee, Lord, I Bow My Head," *Hymns*, no. 158.

. . . . . . . . . . . . . . . . . . . . . . . . . . . . . . .

## SUMMARY

Prayer is the vehicle we can use to communicate with our Father in Heaven. We are commanded to pray always unto the Father. We are also commanded to only pray to Him. We can pray either vocally or silently, asking for guidance and strength, confessing our sins, expressing gratitude, and requesting specific blessings. We should pray individually and as families each day. God answers our prayers by granting us increased ability or by inspiring others to help us. As we pray, we draw closer to our Heavenly Father until our will is the same as His.

One of the most powerful truths we can know is that the Creator of the universe knows and loves us personally. Prayer enables us to talk to our Father who is in heaven as if He were speaking with us face-to-face here on earth. How wonderful it is, not only that God truly hears our prayers, but that He wants to hear them. Inspired lives include daily personal prayer, family prayer, and, if we are married, companionship prayer. All our prayers should be filled with active listening.

## QUOTES

🔹 "Prayer is a supernal gift of our Father in Heaven to every soul. Think of it: the absolute Supreme Being, the most all-knowing, all-seeing, all-powerful personage, encourages you and me, as insignificant as we are, to converse with Him as our Father." (Richard G. Scott, "Using the Supernal Gift of Prayer," *Ensign*, May 2007.)

🔹 "A key to improved prayer is to learn to ask the right questions. Consider changing from asking for the things you want to honestly seeking what He wants for you. Then as you learn His will, pray that you will be led to have the strength to fulfill it." (Richard G. Scott, "Using the Supernal Gift of Prayer," *Ensign*, May 2007.)

🔹 "Our Father in Heaven has promised us peace in times of trial and has provided a way for us to come to Him in our need. He has given us the privilege and power of prayer." (Rex D. Pinegar, "Peace through Prayer," *Ensign,* May 1993.)

🔹 "Men and women of integrity, character, and purpose have ever recognized a power higher than themselves and have sought through prayer to be guided by that power." (Thomas S. Monson, "The Prayer of Faith," *Ensign,* May 1978.)

## ART

Daniel in the Lions' Den, no. 26
Jesus Praying in Gethsemane, no. 56
Enos Praying, no. 72
Moroni Hides the Plates in the Hill Cumorah, no. 86
The First Vision, no. 90
Young Boy Praying, no. 111
Family Prayer, no. 112

## VIDEOS

"And My Soul Hungered": www.lds.org/media-library/video/2012-08-1710-and-my-soul-hungered

"How God Talks to Us Today": www.lds.org/media-library/video/2010-05-1120-how-god-talks-to-us-today

"Pray in Your Families": www.lds.org/media-library/video/2012-08-2900-pray-in-your-families

"Prayer": www.lds.org/media-library/video/2010-01-01-prayer

"Prayer—Sue": www.lds.org/media-library/video/2009-04-101-prayer
-sue?category=topics/prayer

"President Monson Talks about Prayer": www.lds.org/media-library
/video/2011-10-66-president-monson-talks-about-prayer

## OBJECT LESSONS

- Invite the class to share their experiences of trying to find a moment in their hectic lives for personal prayer. Before the discussion, privately ask a sister to continually raise her hand during this sharing moment. Let her know that you will purposely ignore her. You might decide to acknowledge her but tell her you need to say a few more things before she can talk. Finally, when you call on her, have her tell the class what your plan had been. Then explain that sometimes our prayers are like that; we do all of the talking and don't let the Lord participate in the discussion!

- As you walk into the room, talk loudly on your mobile phone as if you are talking to a friend. Talk about your plans for the day, the things you need to do, and then ask for advice. Ask the class to compare your conversation to prayer. Remind them that talking on a cell phone is different from prayer in the following ways:

  - God is never out of range
  - We never "lose the signal"
  - The battery never dies
  - We never run out of minutes
  - God is never too busy to talk
  - We don't need to remember God's number—we just need to talk

- Ask the class to take several long deep breaths. (There are various breathing exercises you can find online that you could have the sisters do for a few minutes.) We need to breathe to stay alive. When we breathe, we inhale oxygen and exhale carbon dioxide. Breathing actually cleanses us. Just as breathing can cleanse our physical bodies, prayer can cleanse our spiritual bodies. Prayer can be a lot like breathing; we need to pray to stay spiritually alive. Paul states in 1 Thessalonians 5:17 that we are to "pray without ceasing." We can't live if our breathing ceases. Neither can our spirits live if our praying ceases.

• • • • • • • • • • • • • • • • • • • • • • • • • • • • • • • •

## ARTICLES

David A. Bednar, "Pray Always," *Ensign*, November 2008.

Dallin H. Oaks, "The Language of Prayer," *Ensign*, May 1993.

Russell M. Nelson, "Lessons from the Lord's Prayers," *Ensign*, May 2009.

James E. Faust, "The Lifeline of Prayer," *Ensign*, May 2002.

N. Eldon Tanner "Importance and Efficacy of Prayer," *Ensign*, August 1971.

Spencer W. Kimball, "Pray Always," *Ensign*, October 1981.

• • • • • • • • • • • • • • • • • • • • • • • • • • • • • • • •

## CHALLENGE

Say a prayer today without asking for anything; just give thanks to the Lord. Offer another prayer tomorrow, this time focusing on other people's needs and how you could help them. Don't mention any of your needs. (Heavenly Father already knows about them anyway!) Write in your journal about those two conversations with Heavenly Father.

• • • • • • • • • • • • • • • • • • • • • • • • • • • • • • • •

## DOCTRINAL MASTERY PASSAGES

- 2 Nephi 32:8–9
- James 1:5–6
- D&C 8:2–3

• • • • • • • • • • • • • • • • • • • • • • • • • • • • • • • •

## *PREACH MY GOSPEL*

38, 73, 93–95

• • • • • • • • • • • • • • • • • • • • • • • • • • • • • • • •

## NOTES

_____

_____

_____

_____

_____

*A key to improved prayer is to learn to ask the right questions. Consider changing from asking for the things you want to honestly seeking what He wants for you. Then as you learn His will, pray that you will be led to have the strength to fulfill it.*

Richard G. Scott, "Using the Supernal Gift of Prayer," *Ensign*, May 2007

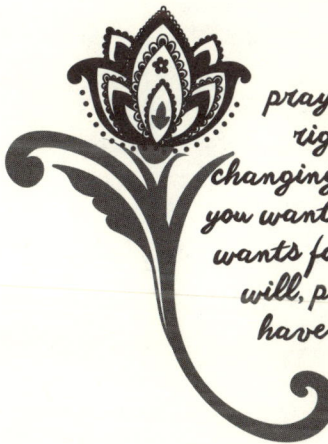

*A key to improved prayer is to learn to ask the right questions. Consider changing from asking for the things you want to honestly seeking what He wants for you. Then as you learn His will, pray that you will be led to have the strength to fulfill it.*

Richard G. Scott, "Using the Supernal Gift of Prayer," *Ensign*, May 2007

*A key to improved prayer is to learn to ask the right questions. Consider changing from asking for the things you want to honestly seeking what He wants for you. Then as you learn His will, pray that you will be led to have the strength to fulfill it.*

Richard G. Scott, "Using the Supernal Gift of Prayer," *Ensign*, May 2007

# *Chapter Seven*

# THE WHISPERINGS OF THE SPIRIT

## MUSIC

"The Holy Ghost," *Children's Songbook*, 105.
"The Still Small Voice," *Children's Songbook*, 106.
"The Spirit of God," *Hymns*, no. 2.
"Great Is the Lord," *Hymns*, no. 77.
"Dearest Children, God Is Near You," *Hymns*, no. 96.

## SUMMARY

The Holy Ghost has been sent to us by a loving Heavenly Father to provide comfort and guidance and to stand as a witness for truth. The Holy Ghost is a member of the Godhead and has a distinct mission to testify of the Father and the Son to our minds and hearts. The Holy Ghost is a personage of spirit that speaks to our souls and by His power we are able to understand and live the gospel of Jesus Christ.

Everyone in the world can feel the influence of the Holy Ghost at certain times; however, the *gift* of the Holy Ghost is the privilege to receive its constant companionship and guidance by the laying on of hands. The gift of the Holy Ghost is bestowed upon a repentant person whose sins have been washed away at baptism. To hear the quiet promptings of the Holy Ghost, we must be obedient, humble, and prayerful. This great gift from a loving Father can bless us with guidance and comfort and can strengthen our testimony.

## QUOTES

● "The simplicity of this ordinance may cause us to overlook its significance. These four words—'Receive the Holy Ghost'—are not a passive pronouncement; rather, they constitute a priesthood injunction—an authoritative admonition to act and not simply to be acted upon." (David A. Bednar, "Receive the Holy Ghost," *Ensign*, November 2010.)

* "We need the help of the Holy Ghost if we are to make our way safely through what the Apostle Paul called the 'perilous times' in which we now live." (Gerald N. Lund, "Opening Our Hearts," *Ensign*, May 2008.)

* "When the Prophet Joseph Smith was asked 'wherein [the LDS Church] differed . . . from the other religions of the day,' he replied that it was in 'the gift of the Holy Ghost by the laying on of hands." (James E. Faust, "The Light in their Eyes," *Ensign*, November 2005.)

* "The Holy Ghost . . . is our comforter, our direction finder, our communicator, our interpreter, our witness, and our purifier—our infallible guide and sanctifier." (Dallin H. Oaks, "'Always Have His Spirit,'" *Ensign*, November 1996.)

* "Testimony brings to us a knowledge that the gospel is true, but conversion by the Spirit brings something more." (Loren C. Dunn, "Fire and the Holy Ghost," *Ensign*, June 1995.)

* "If [we] would open [our] hearts to the refining influence of this unspeakable gift of the Holy Ghost, a glorious new spiritual dimension would come to light." (Joseph B. Wirthlin, "The Unspeakable Gift," *Ensign*, May 2003.)

## ART

Boy Samuel Called by the Lord, no. 18
John the Baptist Baptizing Jesus, no. 35
The Liahona, no. 68
Enos Praying, no. 72
Abinadi before King Noah, no. 75
Samuel the Lamanite on the Wall, no. 81
The Gift of the Holy Ghost, no. 105

## VIDEOS

"The Unspeakable Gift of the Holy Ghost": www.lds.org/media
-library/video/2012-01-0010-the-unspeakable-gift-of-the-holy-ghost

"Feeling the Holy Ghost": www.lds.org/media-library/video/2012-01
-001-feeling-the-holy-ghost
"Having the Holy Ghost": www.lds.org/media-library/video/2012-01
-005-having-the-holy-ghost
There is an excellent three-part series titled "Patterns of Light" by
Elder David A. Bednar available on www.lds.org.

## OBJECT LESSONS

🔆 Have the class listen to sound clips of the voices of the prophets and apostles and try to guess whose voices they hear. Then play some sound clips of the voices of some of the sisters' family members. Talk about how it is much easier to recognize a voice when you are familiar with it. We need to spend time in the scriptures and in prayer in order to recognize the voice of the Lord through the Holy Ghost.

🔆 Demonstrate the difference between the Holy Ghost and the *gift* of the Holy Ghost by using a flashlight. Everyone in the world can feel flashes of inspiration from the Holy Ghost when they are receiving comfort, guidance, or a witness of truth; however, inspiration often quickly fades away. Turn the flashlight on and off. After you are baptized and given the *gift* of the Holy Ghost you have the privilege of having the Holy Ghost as a constant companion. Turn the flashlight on and keep it on. We can keep our "spiritual batteries" charged and receive continuous light from the Holy Ghost if we live worthily.

🔆 Before class, fill one clear glass with water and another with hydrogen peroxide. The glasses should look the same. Ask for a volunteer to dip one index finger into one glass and her other index finger into the other glass. Now ask the volunteer to rub her fingers with each separate hand until her fingers are dry. One should look normal, while the other one should have some white streaks on it (from the hydrogen peroxide). Ask the class "What is the chemical formula for water?" ($H_2O$.) "What is the chemical formula for hydrogen peroxide?" ($H_2O_2$.) How much difference does one oxygen molecule make? The water represents how the Holy Ghost can be with you at times and the hydrogen peroxide represents how the *gift* of the Holy Ghost can stay with you.

## ARTICLES

Douglas L. Callister, "Seeking the Spirit of God," *Ensign*, November 2000.

Neal A. Maxwell, "The Holy Ghost: Glorifying Christ," *Ensign*, July 2002.

James E. Faust, "Communion with the Holy Spirit," *Ensign*, March 2002.

Loren C. Dunn, "Fire and the Holy Ghost," *Ensign*, June 1995.

Boyd K. Packer, "The Gift of the Holy Ghost: What Every Member Should Know," *Ensign*, August 2006.

David A. Bednar, "That We May Always Have His Spirit to Be with Us," *Ensign*, May 2006.

James E. Faust, "The Gift of the Holy Ghost—A Sure Compass," *Ensign*, May 1989.

## CHALLENGE

In Doctrine and Covenants 8:2, the Lord gives us a pattern to help us recognize the Holy Ghost: "Yea, behold, I will tell you in your mind and in your heart, by the Holy Ghost, which shall come upon you and which shall dwell in your heart." Begin a "spiritual journal" where you record your spiritual experiences when you feel the Holy Ghost in your life.

## DOCTRINAL MASTERY PASSAGES

* 2 Nephi 32:3
* Moroni 10:4–5
* James 1:5–6
* D&C 8:2–3
* D&C 130:22–23

## *PREACH MY GOSPEL*

18, 90–91

## NOTES

TESTIMONY BRINGS TO US A
KNOWLEDGE THAT THE GOSPEL IS TRUE,
BUT CONVERSION BY THE SPIRIT BRINGS
SOMETHING MORE.

LOREN C. DUNN, "FIRE AND THE HOLY GHOST,"
*ENSIGN*, JUNE 1995

TESTIMONY BRINGS TO US A
KNOWLEDGE THAT THE GOSPEL IS TRUE,
BUT CONVERSION BY THE SPIRIT BRINGS
SOMETHING MORE.

LOREN C. DUNN, "FIRE AND THE HOLY GHOST,"
*ENSIGN*, JUNE 1995

TESTIMONY BRINGS TO US A
KNOWLEDGE THAT THE GOSPEL IS TRUE,
BUT CONVERSION BY THE SPIRIT BRINGS
SOMETHING MORE.

LOREN C. DUNN, "FIRE AND THE HOLY GHOST,"
*ENSIGN*, JUNE 1995

# Chapter Eight

## WE LOOK TO CHRIST

### MUSIC

"I'm Trying to Be like Jesus," *Children's Songbook*, 78.
"The Lord Is My Light," *Hymns*, no. 89.
"Jesus, Lover of My Soul," *Hymns*, no. 102.
"Come unto Jesus," *Hymns*, no. 117.
"I Know That My Redeemer Lives," *Hymns*, no. 136.
"Jesus, the Very Thought of Thee," *Hymns*, no. 141.

### SUMMARY

We believe in Jesus Christ! Jesus Christ is the Only Begotten Son of God and the Savior of the world. He was chosen and foreordained to come to earth to atone for our sins and teach us how to return to our Heavenly Father. Our faith and hope are built upon the Savior's atoning sacrifice.

The most important events in the history of humankind were when the Savior performed the Atonement and Crucifixion for the world. Jesus performed these acts in the Garden of Gethsemane and on the cross at Calvary. His redeeming sacrifice was necessary to ransom all people from the physical and spiritual effects of sin. Because of His merciful gift, everyone has the opportunity to repent, be forgiven of his or her sins, and be resurrected.

To thank Him for paying our spiritual and physical debts, we must show faith in Him, repent, be baptized, and follow Him. By following Jesus Christ, we can receive peace in this life and eternal joy in the life to come. We can build a testimony of Him through scripture study, prayer, and following His example.

## QUOTES

🌼 "The Christ-centered life produces in us, not a woeful countenance, but a disciplined enthusiasm to work righteousness." (Neal A. Maxwell, "The Christ-Centered Life," *Ensign*, August 1981.)

🌼 "I bear witness that obedience to the gospel plan is the only way to build a Christ-centered life." (Merrill J. Bateman, "Living a Christ-Centered Life," *Ensign*, January 1999.)

🌼 "In this, the dispensation of the fulness of time, as we prepare for the final satanic battles in anticipation of the return of Christ to the earth, it is very important to know who is on the Lord's side. The Lord needs to know on whom He can rely." (Robert C. Oaks, "Who's on the Lord's Side? Who?," *Ensign*, May 2005.)

🌼 "If you will remain on the Lord's side of the line, the adversary cannot come there to tempt you." (George Albert Smith quoted in Charles W. Dahlquist II, "Who's on the Lord's Side?," *Ensign*, May 2007.)

🌼 "The Lord has left no doubt in defining His side and where the Saints should be in their thoughts, words, actions, and practices. We have His counsel in the scriptures and in the words of the prophets." (Joseph B. Wirthlin, "The Lord's Side," *Ensign*, March 1993.)

🌼 "To follow Christ is to become more like Him. It is to learn from His character. As spirit children of our Heavenly Father, we do have the potential to incorporate Christlike attributes into our life and character." (Dieter F. Uchtdorf, "Developing Christlike Attributes," *Ensign*, October 2008.)

• • • • • • • • • • • • • • • • • • • • • • • • • • • • • • • • • • •

## ART

City of Zion Is Taken Up, no. 6
Building the Ark, no. 7
Daniel Refusing the King's Food and Wine, no. 23
Daniel in the Lions' Den, no. 26
The Birth of Jesus, no. 30
Jesus Praying with His Mother, no. 33
Boy Jesus in the Temple, no. 34
John the Baptist Baptizing Jesus, no. 35
Calling of the Fishermen, no. 37
The Sermon on the Mount, no. 39

Jesus Calms the Storm, no. 40

Jesus Raising Jairus's Daughter, no. 41

Christ Healing the Sick at Bethesda, no. 42

Jesus Walking on the Water, no. 43

Mary and Martha, no. 45

Christ and the Children, no. 47

Triumphal Entry, no. 50

Jesus Washing the Apostles' Feet, no. 55

Jesus Praying in Gethsemane, no. 56

The Crucifixion, no. 57

Burial of Jesus, no. 58

Mary and the Resurrected Jesus Christ, no. 59

Jesus Shows His Wounds, no. 60

Go Ye Therefore, no. 61

The Ascension of Jesus, no. 62

Jesus at the Door, no. 65

The Second Coming, no. 66

Captain Moroni Raises the Title of Liberty, no. 79

Two Thousand Young Warriors, no. 80

Jesus Teaching in the Western Hemisphere, no. 82

Jesus Blesses the Nephite Children, no. 84

Girl Being Baptized, no. 104

Young Boy Praying, no. 111

Family Prayer, no. 112

Young Couple Going to the Temple, no. 120

Latter-day Prophets, nos. 122–37

## VIDEOS

"What Is Discipleship?": www.lds.org/media-library/video/2012-01
-8620-what-is-discipleship

"Bible Videos—The Life of Jesus Christ" (a collection of videos of the
Savior's life): www.lds.org/media-library/video/bible-videos-the-life
-of-jesus-christ

"Choose This Day": www.lds.org/media-library/video/2009-09-37
-choose-this-day

"Answers to Life's Great Questions": www.lds.org/media-library
/video/2009-01-58-answers-to-lifes-great-questions

## OBJECT LESSONS

🌸 Bring some fabric squares for the sisters to take home and create their own banners like Captain Moroni's "Title of Liberty." Encourage them to use fabric markers to write how they look to Christ each day.

🌸 Get a picture of Jesus Christ where He is in the center and other items or people are surrounding Him. Cut it up into puzzle pieces, and invite the sisters to put it together. Notice that once you put Christ in the center, the rest of the puzzle is easier to solve.

🌸 Show various pictures that represent sources of light: the sun, solar panel, flashlight, candle, porch light, spotlight, lighthouse, fireplace, night-light, and so on. Talk about their unique purposes and then show a picture of the Savior. Compare and contrast His purpose to those of the other light sources.

🌸 What is at the center of our daily lives? More to the point, *who* is our life centered on? Our challenge during mortality is to choose the eternal kingdom of God rather than temporary earthly glory. What good is having someone who can walk on water if you don't follow in His footsteps? Set out pictures that represent the life of Christ. Invite the sisters to choose one and share what it means to them.

## ARTICLES

Richard J. Maynes, "Establishing a Christ-Centered Home," *Ensign*, May 2011.

Lawrence E. Corbridge, "Valiant in the Testimony of Jesus Christ," *Ensign*, September 2011.

Clate W. Mask Jr., "Standing Spotless before the Lord," *Ensign*, May 2004.

Stephen A. West, "Are You on the Lord's Side?," *New Era*, September 2002.

Bernard P. Brockbank, "Knowing God," *Ensign*, July 1972.

N. Eldon Tanner, "A Basis for Faith in the Living God," *Ensign*, November 1978.

## CHALLENGE

Look at the Christlike qualities listed in the "Attribute Activity" on page 126 of *Preach My Gospel*. Evaluate how you are doing in developing those characteristics. (Do the activity to determine which characteristics you're struggling with the most and that you need to work on in your life.) Create a plan of action for how you will make Christ more central in your daily thoughts and actions.

## DOCTRINAL MASTERY PASSAGES

- 2 Nephi 32:3
- Helaman 5:12
- Moroni 10:4–5
- Exodus 20:3–17
- Joshua 24:15
- Proverbs 3:5–6
- Isaiah 53:3–5
- Daniel 2:44
- Luke 24:36–39
- John 14:15
- John 17:3
- Ephesians 4:11–14
- Revelation 20:12
- Joseph Smith—History 1:15–20
- D&C 76:22–24

## PREACH MY GOSPEL

1, 5, 33, 37, 46, 48, 51–54, 60–61, 90, 105, 108, 115–16, 123–26, 198–99

## NOTES

_____
_____
_____
_____
_____
_____
_____
_____
_____
_____

I bear witness that obedience to the gospel plan is the only way to build a Christ-centered life.

MERRILL J. BATEMAN, "LIVING A CHRIST-CENTERED LIFE," *ENSIGN*, JANUARY 1999

I bear witness that obedience to the gospel plan is the only way to build a Christ-centered life.

MERRILL J. BATEMAN, "LIVING A CHRIST-CENTERED LIFE," *ENSIGN*, JANUARY 1999

I bear witness that obedience to the gospel plan is the only way to build a Christ-centered life.

MERRILL J. BATEMAN, "LIVING A CHRIST-CENTERED LIFE," *ENSIGN*, JANUARY 1999

# Chapter Nine

## THE PRECIOUS GIFT OF TESTIMONY

### MUSIC

"Faith of Our Fathers," *Hymns*, no. 84.
"Come unto Jesus," *Hymns*, no. 117.
"When Faith Endures," *Hymns*, no. 128.
"True to the Faith," *Hymns*, no. 254.
"Go Forth with Faith," *Hymns*, no. 263.

### SUMMARY

As we exercise faith in the Lord, live His commandments, and pray for His guidance, we gain a testimony of Him and His gospel. Elder Dallin H. Oaks described a testimony as "a personal witness borne to our souls by the Holy Ghost"—a testimony "that certain facts of eternal significance are true and that we know them to be true" ("Testimony," *Ensign*, May 2008). As we live gospel principles, we are testing those principles in our lives and gaining knowledge that they are truths that have blessed our lives.

### QUOTES

- "Honestly acknowledge your questions and your concerns, but first and forever fan the flame of your faith, because all things are possible to them that believe." (Jeffrey R. Holland, "Lord, I Believe" *Ensign*, May 2013.)

- "It is not enough to know that God lives, that Jesus Christ is our Savior, and that the gospel is true. We must take the high road by acting upon that knowledge." (Dallin H. Oaks, "Be Not Deceived," *Ensign*, November 2004.)

"This is my prayer for all of us—'Lord, increase our faith.' Increase our faith to bridge the chasms of uncertainty and doubt. . . . Grant us faith to look beyond the problems of the moment to the miracles of the future. . . . Give us faith to do what is right and let the consequence follow." (Gordon B. Hinckley, "'Lord, Increase Our Faith,'" *Ensign*, November 1987.)

"We promote the process of strengthening our faith when we do what is right—increased faith always follows." (L. Whitney Clayton, "'Help Thou Mine Unbelief,'" *Ensign*, November 2001.)

"Faith in Jesus Christ takes us beyond mere acceptance of the Savior's identity and existence. It includes having complete confidence in His infinite and eternal redemptive power." (James O. Mason, "Faith in Jesus Christ," *Ensign*, April 2001.)

## ART

Jesus Christ, no. 1
Abraham Taking Isaac to Be Sacrificed, no. 9
The Ten Commandments, no. 14
Moses and the Brass Serpent, no. 16
Three Men in the Fiery Furnace, no. 25
Daniel in the Lions' Den, no. 26
Jesus Raising Jairus's Daughter, no. 41
Christ Healing the Sick at Bethesda, no. 42
Jesus Praying in Gethsemane, no. 56
The Crucifixion, no. 57
Jesus Shows His Wounds, no. 60
Jesus at the Door, no. 65
Enos Praying, no. 72
Conversion of Alma the Younger, no. 77
Two Thousand Young Warriors, no. 80
The Brother of Jared Sees the Finger of the Lord, no. 85

## VIDEOS

"Transforming Power of Faith and Character": www.lds.org/media
-library/video/2015-00-006-transforming-power-of-faith-and
-character

"We Believe: Theme Song": www.lds.org/media-library/video/2010-12
-02-we-believe-theme-son
"Finding Faith in Christ": www.lds.org/media-library/video/2004-01
-01-finding-faith-in-christ
"Waiting on Our Road to Damascus": www.lds.org/media-library
/video/2012-01-003-waiting-on-our-road-to-damascus

## OBJECT LESSONS

- At the end of this book is a list of websites that have free clip art available. Go to some of the websites and print off a few clip art pages that apply to this lesson's content. Invite sisters to color pictures while they listen to the lesson and discuss the principles. Encourage them to use the pictures in a future family home evening lesson.

- Show the class a checkerboard with 1 grain of wheat on the first square, 2 on the second, 4 on the third, 8, 16, 32, 64, 128, and so on. Ask the class "At this rate of doubling every square, how many grains would you have on the checkerboard by the time you reach the sixty-fourth square?" Let the class guess and tell them the correct answer is enough grain to cover the entire subcontinent of India fifty feet deep with grain. Each square represents some area of their life where they need to trust God. Talk about how our faith may start out small, but as we exercise it, the end result can be miraculous and quite powerful.

- Pass out some small jars (baby food jars) filled with whipping cream. Ask the class if they have faith that the cream can turn into butter. Explain that real faith is more than belief—it should lead to action. Have the class shake the jars during the lesson until the cream turns into sweet butter. Explain how building a testimony requires time, work, and patience. Before the lesson is over, pass out blueberry muffins for the sisters to eat with the butter.

## ARTICLES

Gordon B. Hinckley, "Faith: The Essence of True Religion," *Ensign*, October 1995.
Russell M. Nelson, "Faith in Jesus Christ," *Ensign*, March 2008.
Henry B. Eyring, "Testimony and Conversion," *Ensign*, February 2015.

Robert D. Hales, "Finding Faith in the Lord Jesus Christ," *Ensign*, November 2004.

Robert D. Hales, "General Conference: Strengthening Faith and Testimony," *Ensign*, November 2013.

• • • • • • • • • • • • • • • • • • • • • • • • • • • • • • • • • •

## CHALLENGE

Write a list of everything that builds your faith. Begin doing one of the things on your list that you haven't included in your daily life lately.

• • • • • • • • • • • • • • • • • • • • • • • • • • • • • • • • • •

## DOCTRINAL MASTERY PASSAGES

- 2 Nephi 2:27
- Alma 41:10
- Ether 12:6
- Genesis 39:9
- Exodus 20:3–17
- Psalm 24:3–4
- Proverbs 3:5–6

- Isaiah 1:18
- John 14:15
- James 1:5–6
- James 2:17–18
- D&C 19:16–19
- D&C 58:42–43

• • • • • • • • • • • • • • • • • • • • • • • • • • • • • • • • • •

## PREACH MY GOSPEL

49–50, 62–63, 93–95, 155, 187–90, 195

• • • • • • • • • • • • • • • • • • • • • • • • • • • • • • • • • •

## NOTES

_____

_____

_____

_____

_____

_____

_____

_____

This is my prayer for all of us—"Lord, increase our faith." Increase our faith to bridge the chasms of uncertainty and doubt. . . . Grant us faith to look beyond the problems of the moment to the miracles of the future. . . . Give us faith to do what is right and let the consequence follow.

GORDON B. HINCKLEY, "LORD, INCREASE OUR FAITH," *ENSIGN*, NOVEMBER 1987

This is my prayer for all of us—"Lord, increase our faith." Increase our faith to bridge the chasms of uncertainty and doubt. . . . Grant us faith to look beyond the problems of the moment to the miracles of the future. . . . Give us faith to do what is right and let the consequence follow.

GORDON B. HINCKLEY, "LORD, INCREASE OUR FAITH," *ENSIGN*, NOVEMBER 1987

# *Chapter Ten*

## NURTURING THE ETERNAL PARTNERSHIP OF MARRIAGE

• • • • • • • • • • • • • • • • • • • • • • • • • • • • • • • • • • • • • •

### MUSIC

"O My Father," *Hymns*, no. 292.
"Home Can Be a Heaven on Earth," *Hymns*, no. 298.
"I Am a Child of God," *Hymns*, no. 301.
"Teach Me to Walk in the Light," *Hymns*, no. 304.

• • • • • • • • • • • • • • • • • • • • • • • • • • • • • • • • • • • • • •

### SUMMARY

Marriage is ordained of God between a man and a woman. Temple marriage is a sacred partnership with you, your spouse, and God. It is essential for exaltation, which is the perfect union of man and woman. Temple marriage is a covenant partnership with the Lord that allows us to seal souls together as eternal families.

Celestial marriage is the crowning ordinance of the gospel of Jesus Christ. The benefits of a temple marriage are not just eternal, but temporal as well. Joy in marriage grows sweeter as husband and wife both remain faithful and obedient to gospel covenants.

Be sensitive to the sisters in the class who may have never married, never been sealed, lost a spouse, or been divorced. Remind them that the Lord has promised a fulness of blessings to all those who are faithful.

• • • • • • • • • • • • • • • • • • • • • • • • • • • • • • • • • • • • • •

### QUOTES

❧ "To those who keep the covenant of marriage, God promises the fulness of His glory, eternal lives, eternal increase, exaltation in the celestial kingdom, and a fulness of joy." (F. Burton Howard, "Eternal Marriage," *Ensign*, May 2003.)

🍂 "Marriage between a man and a woman is ordained of God, and only through the new and everlasting covenant of marriage can we realize the fulness of all eternal blessings." (David E. Sorensen, "The Honeymoon Trail," *Liahona,* October 1997.)

🍂 "Temple marriage is a covenant that bridges death, transcends time, stretches unbreakable into eternity." (Spencer W. Kimball, "First Presidency Message: Temples and Eternal Marriage," *Ensign,* August 1974.)

🍂 "A successful marriage requires falling in love many times, always with the same person." (Mignon McLaughlin, *The Complete Neurotic's Notebook* [Castle Books, 1981].)

🍂 "I am satisfied that a happy marriage is not so much a matter of romance as it is an anxious concern for the comfort and well-being of one's companion." (Gordon B. Hinckley, "What God Hath Joined Together," *Ensign*, May 1991.)

## ART

Adam and Eve Kneeling at an Altar, no. 4
Adam and Eve Teaching Their Children, no. 5
Jacob Blessing His Sons, no. 12
Lehi's Dream, no. 69
Elijah Appearing in the Kirtland Temple, no. 95
Young Couple Going to the Temple, no. 120

## VIDEOS

"Families Can Be Together Forever": www.lds.org/media-library/video/2011-02-001-families-can-be-together-forever?category=topics/marriage-and-family

"Highlight: Why Marriage and Family Matters—Everywhere in the World": www.lds.org/media-library/video/2015-04-160-elder-l-tom-perry-highlights

"What Is the Purpose of Family?": www.lds.org/media-library/video/topics/marriage-and-family

## OBJECT LESSONS

❦ Have two sisters hold either end of a short string across the front of the room. Now ask another sister to attach a clothespin to the string, except only give her half of a clothespin. She obviously won't be able to attach it. Give her a complete clothespin and allow her to attach it to the string. Now ask another sister to cut the string with scissors, however, only give her one half of the scissors. Obviously, she won't be able to complete the task. Now give her a real pair of scissors and allow her to cut the string. Both items serve as great analogies for marriage. If only one person is trying to hang on, it won't work; you need both partners to work together. Likewise, if both partners in the marriage choose "cutting" remarks and are always fighting, it won't take long for everything to fall apart.

❦ Have a husband and wife play tug-of-war, using a paper chain. The chain represents civil marriage. It doesn't take long to separate if the husband and wife are pulling at opposite ends with different goals. Now ask the same husband and wife to play tug-of-war, this time using a metal chain, which represents temple marriage. With a strong foundation, even if the couple struggles through life they can hold the marriage together.

❦ Hold up a donut and compare it to temporal marriage: sweet and delicious, but built around a big hole—"'til death do us part." Tell the sisters "Do-nut settle for a marriage that won't last into the eternities." Then pass around cinnamon rolls, comparing them to eternal marriage, without a hole.

• • • • • • • • • • • • • • • • • • • • • • • • • • • • • • • • • •

## ARTICLES

Spencer W. Kimball, "The Importance of Celestial Marriage," *Ensign*, October 1979.

Bruce C. Hafen, "Covenant Marriage," *Ensign*, November 1996.

F. Burton Howard, "Eternal Marriage," *Ensign*, May 2003.

Spencer W. Kimball, "First Presidency Message: Temples and Eternal Marriage," *Ensign*, August 1974.

Marion D. Hanks, "Eternal Marriage," *Ensign*, November 1984.

L. Whitney Clayton, "Marriage: Watch and Learn," *Ensign*, May 2013.

## CHALLENGES

- If you are married, write a list of all the good qualities you see in your husband. Refer to this list when you get frustrated with him! Choose one new act of service you will perform for him this week that you've never done before. Plan your next date night.

- If you have never been married, pray for patience. Look online for a singles conference you could attend and invite some friends you could attend it with.

- If you are an older widow, pray for comfort until you and your husband can be reunited. Discover ways you can use your talents to bless others.

## DOCTRINAL MASTERY PASSAGES

- 2 Nephi 2:25
- Moses 1:39
- Genesis 1:26–27
- Genesis 39:9
- Exodus 20:3–17
- D&C 131:1–4

## PREACH MY GOSPEL

3, 31, 47–50, 54, 85–86, 159, 164–65

## NOTES

I am satisfied that
a happy marriage is not
so much a matter of romance
as it is an anxious concern for
the comfort and well-being of
one's companion.

Gordon B. Hinckley, "What God Hath Joined
Together," *Ensign*, May 1991

I am satisfied that
a happy marriage is not
so much a matter of romance
as it is an anxious concern for
the comfort and well-being of
one's companion.

Gordon B. Hinckley, "What God Hath Joined
Together," *Ensign*, May 1991

# *Chapter Eleven*

## HOME—THE BASIS OF A RIGHTEOUS LIFE

. . . . . . . . . . . . . . . . . . . . . . . . . . . . . . . . . . . . . . . . . .

### MUSIC

"O My Father," *Hymns*, no. 292.
"Our Father, by Whose Name," *Hymns*, no. 296.
"Home Can Be a Heaven on Earth," *Hymns*, no. 298.
"Families Can Be Together Forever," *Hymns*, no. 300.
"I Am a Child of God," *Hymns*, no. 301.
"Teach Me to Walk in the Light," *Hymns*, no. 304.

. . . . . . . . . . . . . . . . . . . . . . . . . . . . . . . . . . . . . . . . . .

### SUMMARY

Life is eternal. We come from heavenly parents who are waiting for us to return to them once we have learned the lessons of life and gained the characteristics they possess. To remind us of our heavenly home, we are given the opportunity to be parents here on earth and to raise a family of our own. Salvation is a family affair. The family is the most important unit in time and eternity. We are placed here as families to learn how to care for one another, so that we may all safely return home together. Temple marriage is a covenant partnership with the Lord that allows us to seal souls together as eternal families.

Heavenly Father has placed us here on earth in families so that we can learn to work together and help one another return to our heavenly home, each one playing an important role. Fathers are to provide, protect, and preside over families. Mothers are divinely designed to bear and nurture children. Children are commanded to honor and obey their parents. If everyone takes responsibility for a happy family, they can all experience a little bit of heaven on earth.

Be sensitive to the sisters in the class who may have never married, lost a spouse, or been divorced. Remind them the Lord has promised a fulness of blessings to all those who are faithful.

• • • • • • • • • • • • • • • • • • • • • • • • • • • • • • • • • • •

## QUOTES

🌸 "In light of the ultimate purpose of the great plan of happiness, I believe that the ultimate treasures on earth and in heaven are our children and our posterity." (Dallin H. Oaks, "'The Great Plan of Happiness,'" *Ensign*, November 1993.)

🌸 "Under the plan of heaven, the husband and the wife walk side by side as companions, neither one ahead of the other, but a daughter of God and a son of God walking side by side. Let your families be families of love and peace and happiness. Gather your children around you and have your family home evenings, teach your children the ways of the Lord, read to them from the scriptures, and let them come to know the great truths of the eternal gospel as set forth in these words of the Almighty." (Gordon B. Hinckley, "Latter-day Counsel: Selections from Addresses of President Gordon B. Hinckley," *Ensign,* March 2001.)

🌸 "Our family is the focus of our greatest work and joy in this life; so will it be throughout all eternity." (Russell M. Nelson, "'Set in Order Thy House,'" *Ensign,* November 2001.)

🌸 "The key to strengthening our families is having the Spirit of the Lord come into our homes. The goal of our families is to be on the strait and narrow path." (Robert D. Hales, "Strengthening Families: Our Sacred Duty," *Ensign,* May 1999.)

🌸 "The family unit is fundamental not only to society and to the Church but also to our hope for eternal life." (Henry B. Eyring, "The Family," *Ensign*, February 1998.)

🌸 "Individual progression is fostered in the family, which is 'central to the Creator's plan for the eternal destiny of His children.'" (Russell M. Nelson, "Salvation and Exaltation," *Ensign*, May 2008.)

• • • • • • • • • • • • • • • • • • • • • • • • • • • • • • • • • • •

## ART

Jesus Christ, no. 1
Adam and Eve Kneeling at an Altar, no. 4

Adam and Eve Teaching Their Children, no. 5
Jacob Blessing His Sons, no. 12
Lehi's Dream, no. 69
Elijah Appearing in the Kirtland Temple, no. 95
Young Couple Going to the Temple, no. 120

## VIDEOS

"Until We Meet Again": www.lds.org/media-library/video/2010-05-11
-until-we-meet-again
"The Blessings of the Temple": www.lds.org/media-library/video/2009
-03-10-the-blessings-of-the-temple
"Faith and Families": www.lds.org/media-library/video/2005-02-01
-faith-and-families
"Marriage and Divorce": www.lds.org/media-library/video/2009-07-28
-marriage-and-divorce

## OBJECT LESSONS

🏵 Get two large envelopes. Glue a picture of a temple on the outside of one of them. Ask a volunteer to place paper dolls inside the two envelopes, creating families inside the envelopes. Seal the envelope that has the picture of a temple on the outside. Talk about life's challenges that can tear us apart, then turn the two envelopes upside down, shaking the contents around. The family that has been sealed together will stay together, but the other family will all fall out of the envelope.

🏵 Pass out copies of "The Family: A Proclamation to the World" to give to everyone in the class. Give them the option to color and decorate them during your lesson.

🏵 Place a stalk of celery in a glass of colored water a few days prior to your lesson. The food coloring in the water will actually draw up into the celery! Show the class your visual aid and ask them to draw analogies between the celery, food coloring, and our parenting skills. Children literally soak up what is around them in the home: anger, love, gospel study, apathy, and so on. We need to constantly expose our children to positive behaviors in order for them to absorb the gospel.

## ARTICLES

Robert D. Hales, "The Eternal Family," *Ensign*, November 1996.

Henry B. Eyring, "The Family," *Ensign*, February 1998.

L. Tom Perry, "The Importance of the Family," *Ensign*, May 2003.

Spencer W. Kimball, "Living the Gospel in the Home," *Ensign*, May 1978.

Spencer W. Kimball, "The Importance of Celestial Marriage," *Ensign*, October 1979.

Bruce C. Hafen, "Covenant Marriage," *Ensign*, November 1996.

F. Burton Howard, "Eternal Marriage," *Ensign*, May 2003.

## CHALLENGE

Write down the names of everyone in your family. Make a list of things you can do to serve them and help them reach their personal goals.

## DOCTRINAL MASTERY PASSAGES

- Ether 12:27
- Moroni 7:45
- D&C 131:1–4

## PREACH MY GOSPEL

3, 32, 85, 159–64

## NOTES

_____

_____

_____

_____

_____

_____

_____

_____

Our family is the focus of our
greatest work and joy in this life; so
will it be throughout all eternity.

Russell M. Nelson, "'Set in Order Thy House,'"
*Ensign*, November 2001

Our family is the focus of our
greatest work and joy in this life; so
will it be throughout all eternity.

Russell M. Nelson, "'Set in Order Thy House,'"
*Ensign*, November 2001

# *Chapter Twelve*

## OBEDIENCE—SIMPLY LIVE THE GOSPEL

. . . . . . . . . . . . . . . . . . . . . . . . . . . . . . . .

### MUSIC

"Quickly I'll Obey," *Children's Songbook*, 197.
"Thy Will, O Lord, Be Done," *Hymns*, no. 188.
"Do What Is Right," *Hymns*, no. 237.
"Keep the Commandments," *Hymns*, no. 303.
"How Gentle God's Commands," *Hymns*, no. 314.

. . . . . . . . . . . . . . . . . . . . . . . . . . . . . . . .

### SUMMARY

Because God is our loving Father in Heaven, He knows what is best for our eternal progression and so He gives us commandments to protect us along our earthly journey. In exchange for His guidance, we give Him our obedience. Heavenly Father knows what will make us eternally happy, so commandments are designed to steer us away from things that will harm or destroy us spiritually or physically. Obedience is a measure of our commitment to God. Obeying out of love is better than obeying out of fear.

. . . . . . . . . . . . . . . . . . . . . . . . . . . . . . . .

### QUOTES

🪷 "The Lord has left no doubt in defining His side and where the Saints should be in their thoughts, words, actions, and practices. We have His counsel in the scriptures and in the words of the prophets." (Joseph B. Wirthlin, "The Lord's Side," *Ensign*, March 1993.)

🪷 "You will need the help of heaven to keep the commandments. You will need it more and more as the days go on. . . . But you can bring the protective powers of heaven down on you by simply decid-ing to go toward the Savior, to wait on Him." (Henry B. Eyring, "Waiting Upon the Lord" [Brigham Young University devotional, September 30, 1990]; speeches.byu.edu.)

🌸 "The Book of Mormon, in addition to being another testament of Jesus Christ, is a book about the results of keeping and not keep-ing commandments." (Gregory A. Schwitzer, "Developing Good Judgment and Not Judging Others," *Ensign*, May 2010.)

🌸 "My brothers and sisters, the great test of this life is obedience." (Thomas S. Monson, "Obedience Brings Blessings," *Ensign*, May 2013.)

🌸 "There is no need for you or for me, in this enlightened age when the fulness of the gospel has been restored, to sail uncharted seas or to travel unmarked roads in search of truth. A loving Heavenly Father has plotted our course and provided an unfailing guide—even *obe-dience*. A knowledge of truth and the answers to our greatest ques-tions come to us as we are obedient to the commandments of God." (Thomas S. Monson, "Obedience Brings Blessings," *Ensign*, May 2013; emphasis in original.)

## ART

City of Zion Is Taken Up, no. 6
Building the Ark, no. 7
Abraham Taking Isaac to Be Sacrificed, no. 9
Joseph Resists Potiphar's Wife, no. 11
The Ten Commandments, no. 14
Esther, no. 21
Daniel Refusing the King's Food and Wine, no. 23
Three Men in the Fiery Furnace, no. 25
Daniel in the Lions' Den, no. 26
Jonah, no. 27
John the Baptist Baptizing Jesus, no. 35
The Liahona, no. 68
Alma Baptizes in the Waters of Mormon, no. 76
Two Thousand Young Warriors, no. 80
Young Man Being Baptized, no. 103
Girl Being Baptized, no. 104

## VIDEOS

"Obedience to the Ten Commandments": www.lds.org/media-library
/video/2015-03-002-obedience-to-the-ten-commandments

"Obedience Brings Blessings": www.lds.org/media-library/video/2014
-06-1130-obedience-brings-blessings

"Chapter 9: Abraham and the Sacrifice of Isaac": www.lds.org
/media-library/video/2010-12-09-chapter-9-abraham-and-the
-sacrifice-of-isaac?category=children/old-testament-stories-friend

"Obedience to the Prophets": www.lds.org/media-library/video
/annual-mutual-theme/unit-10-dc

## OBJECT LESSONS

Ask someone to read the recipe for chocolate chip cookies while you make them. When "oil" is mentioned, add some car oil. When "flour" is read aloud, toss some flowers into the bowl. Add potato chips instead of chocolate chips. Instead of baking soda, toss in some soda pop. Use garlic salt when "salt" is mentioned. Of course, by now the class will either be groaning or laughing. Talk about how when the Lord asks us to be obedient, we can't pick and choose how we'll interpret the commandments.

Wrap an egg in Bubble Wrap and tissue and then drop it on the floor. The soft packaging should cushion the egg, which would have broken without the protection. The gospel is designed to protect each of us in the same way—by helping us build layers of testimony as we keep the commandments.

Shine a spotlight on someone. Now ask her to move one step away. Point out that while she may still have a little bit of light shining on her, she does not have as much as before. Now ask her to move five steps away and show that she no longer has any light shining on her. The light is Jesus Christ. He is not the one who moves from us. It only takes one step away from the Lord to reduce His light on us. When we sin without repenting, we are taking more and more steps away from Him. To continue to receive the Lord's illumination in our lives, we can't move—we must stay close to Him and keep the commandments.

## ARTICLES

Thomas S. Monson, "Obedience Brings Blessings," *Ensign*, May 2013.

L. Tom Perry, "Obedience to Law Is Liberty," *Ensign*, May 2013.

L. Tom Perry, "Obedience through Our Faithfulness," *Ensign*, May 2014.

Robert D. Hales, "'If Ye Love Me, Keep My Commandments,'" *Ensign*, May 2014.

Russell Ballard Jr., "Learn Obedience and Service," *Ensign*, May 1976.

## CHALLENGE

Consider one of the commandments that you might not be obeying 100 percent. Ponder why the Lord would give such a commandment. How could you be blessed if you followed the commandment with love for the Lord and strict obedience? How would your life be better? How would your spirituality increase? Decide what you will do to improve your commitment to live that particular commandment.

## DOCTRINAL MASTERY PASSAGES

- 1 Nephi 3:7
- 2 Nephi 2:27
- Exodus 20:3–17
- Isaiah 29:13–14
- John 7:17
- John 14:15
- 2 Timothy 3:15–17
- James 2:17–18
- D&C 1:37–38
- D&C 82:10
- D&C 89:18–21

## *PREACH MY GOSPEL*

1, 19, 72, 75–76, 88, 97, 115, 122–26, 150–51, 168–69

## NOTES

_____

_____

_____

_____

The Book of Mormon, in addition to being another testament of Jesus Christ, is a book about the results of keeping and not keeping commandments.

Gregory A. Schwitzer, "Developing Good Judgment and Not Judging Others," *Ensign*, May 2010

The Book of Mormon, in addition to being another testament of Jesus Christ, is a book about the results of keeping and not keeping commandments.

Gregory A. Schwitzer, "Developing Good Judgment and Not Judging Others," *Ensign*, May 2010

The Book of Mormon, in addition to being another testament of Jesus Christ, is a book about the results of keeping and not keeping commandments.

Gregory A. Schwitzer, "Developing Good Judgment and Not Judging Others," *Ensign*, May 2010

# *Chapter Thirteen*

## PEACE AND CONTENTMENT THROUGH TEMPORAL SELF-RELIANCE

### MUSIC

"I'm Glad to Pay a Tithing," *Children's Songbook*, 150.
"Go the Second Mile," *Children's Songbook*, 167.
"God Is Watching Over All," *Children's Songbook*, 229.
"Great King of Heaven," *Hymns*, no. 63.
"Have I Done Any Good?," *Hymns*, no. 223.
"Put Your Shoulder to the Wheel," *Hymns*, no. 252.
"As Sisters in Zion," *Hymns*, no. 309.

### SUMMARY

A part of this life involves learning how to take care of our bodies and spirits so that we will be better prepared to live an exalted life with our Heavenly Father. Our mortal education includes learning how to provide for both physical and spiritual needs of others and ourselves. A merciful Father in Heaven counsels us through His prophets to be prepared in all things. Everything we have in mortality is a test to see if we are able to be good and faithful stewards of even more in eternity.

Work gives us purpose and helps us provide for our wants and needs. Doing our best work is a matter of integrity, instilling an attitude of honor in all that we do. As mothers, we need to teach our children to work and not rely on others for everything. In order to learn to accept responsibility, children need to see us work, work beside us, and learn to work alone. Idleness is contrary to the gospel.

## QUOTES

🏵 "Self-reliance implies the individual development of skills and abilities and then their application to provide for one's own needs and wants. It further implies that one will achieve those skills through self-discipline and then, through self-restraint and charity, use those skills to bless himself and others." (Marion G. Romney, "Principles of Temporal Salvation," *Ensign*, April 1981.)

🏵 "Inspired prophets have always been given laws for their temporal well-being, as well as knowledge that saves eternally. Likewise, as a prelude to this revelation the Lord placed emphasis on both temporal salvation and spiritual salvation: 'All things unto me are spiritual, and not at any time have I given unto you a law which was temporal . . . for my commandments are spiritual' (D&C 29:34–35)." (Roy W. Doxey, "The Lord's People Blessed by Temporal Law," *Liahona*, October 1983.)

🏵 "The work of caring for one another and being 'kind to the poor' is a sanctifying work, commanded of the Father." (H. David Burton, "The Sanctifying Work of Welfare," *Ensign*, April 2011.)

🏵 "Let us realize that the privilege to work is a gift, that the power to work is a blessing, that love of work is success." (David O. McKay quoted in Franklin D. Richards, "The Gospel of Work," *Improvement Era*, November 1969.)

🏵 "I do not believe people can be happy unless they have work to do. . . . If we learn to work early in life we will be better individuals, better members of families, better neighbors, and better disciples of Jesus Christ, who Himself learned to work as a carpenter." (Neal A. Maxwell, "Friend to Friend: Gospel of Work," *Friend*, June 1975.)

## ART

Building the Ark, no. 7
Noah and the Ark with Animals, no. 8
Jesus Praying with His Mother, no. 33
Jesus Raising Jairus's Daughter, no. 41
Christ Healing the Sick at Bethesda, no. 42
The Good Samaritan, no. 44
Mary and Martha, no. 45

Christ and the Rich Young Ruler, no. 48
Lehi and His People Arrive in the Promised Land, no. 71
Ammon Defends the Flocks of King Lamoni, no. 78
Emma Crossing the Ice, no. 96
Handcart Pioneers Approaching the Salt Lake Valley, no. 102
Service, no. 115

## VIDEOS

"Providing in the Lord's Way": www.lds.org/media-library/video
/2011-07-364-providing-in-the-lords-way
"The Errand of Angels": www.lds.org/media-library/video/2011-07
-078-the-errand-of-angels
"Seek the Higher Ground": www.lds.org/media-library/video/2010-04
-09-seek-the-higher-ground
"Caring for the Poor and Needy": www.lds.org/media-library/video
/2013-02-2010-caring-for-the-poor-and-needy
"The Labor of His Hands": www.lds.org/media-library/video/2011-05
-09-the-labor-of-his-hands
There are numerous videos that address various aspects of self-reliance
at www.lds.org/media-library/video/categories/pef-self-reliance.

## OBJECT LESSONS

Hold up a wire clothes hanger and ask what it is used for. Ask if anyone can name other uses for a wire hanger. They might make suggestions such as opening a locked car door, roasting marshmallows, cleaning a clogged drain, craft projects, and so on.
Read Doctrine and Covenants 60:2 and 82:18. Ask the group what these scriptures have to do with the hanger. Remind everyone that the Lord expects us to do more than just "hang around." Challenge them to list ways they can use their talents to bless others spiritually and temporally.

Set out three boxes on the table in the front of the classroom. Ask three volunteers to each choose a box, but only if they are willing to accept responsibility for it. In one box is a bottle of glass cleaner, requiring the volunteer to wash the window in the classroom. Another box has a bottle of lemon oil, which the volunteer has to use to dust the table or piano in the room. The third box contains a candy bar, which the volunteer gets to eat and enjoy! Explain that we all have our agency to make choices, but once we have made a choice, we are committed to it, whether it is fun or not.

🌀 Show a dry sponge. How good is it at cleaning? First it soaks up everything, which is how we are when we are learning about the gospel and provident living principles. Once we are filled, we can then "ooze" those things to others. Our testimonies and service can easily flow to others once we have learned them for ourselves.

## ARTICLES

Gordon B. Hinckley, "Life's Obligations," *Ensign*, February 1999.

Marion G. Romney, "Principles of Temporal Salvation," *Ensign*, April 1981.

Roy W. Doxey, "The Lord's People Blessed by Temporal Law," *Tambuli*, October 1983.

H. David Burton, "The Sanctifying Work of Welfare," *Liahona*, May 2011.

Spencer W. Kimball, "Welfare Services: The Gospel in Action," *Ensign*, November 1977.

## CHALLENGE

Gather items that can be donated to someone in need: food, clothing, household appliances, books, diapers, and so on. There are many organizations that would gladly accept your donations: Deseret Industries, The Salvation Army, local food banks or women's shelters, Goodwill Industries, Vietnam Veterans of America, United Way, and so on.

## DOCTRINAL MASTERY PASSAGES

- 1 Nephi 3:7
- Mosiah 2:17
- Moroni 7:45
- Moses 1:39
- Moses 7:18
- Exodus 20:3–17
- Joshua 24:15
- Psalm 24:3–4
- Proverbs 3:5–6
- Malachi 3:8–10
- Matthew 5:14–16
- Ephesians 4:11–14
- 2 Timothy 3:16–17
- James 2:17–18
- D&C 89:18–21

## *PREACH MY GOSPEL*

3, 8, 19, 23, 31, 50, 66, 87–88, 107, 119, 121, 137, 144–53, 168–69, 188–89

• • • • • • • • • • • • • • • • • • • • • • • • • • • • • • • • • • • •

## NOTES

_____

_____

_____

_____

_____

_____

_____

_____

_____

_____

_____

_____

_____

_____

_____

_____

_____

_____

_____

_____

_____

> I DO NOT BELIEVE PEOPLE CAN BE HAPPY UNLESS THEY HAVE WORK TO DO. . . . IF WE LEARN TO WORK EARLY IN LIFE WE WILL BE BETTER INDIVIDUALS, BETTER MEMBERS OF FAMILIES, BETTER NEIGHBORS, AND BETTER DISCIPLES OF JESUS CHRIST, WHO HIMSELF LEARNED TO WORK AS A CARPENTER.
>
> NEAL A. MAXWELL, "FRIEND TO FRIEND: GOSPEL OF WORK," *FRIEND*, JUNE 1975

> I DO NOT BELIEVE PEOPLE CAN BE HAPPY UNLESS THEY HAVE WORK TO DO. . . . IF WE LEARN TO WORK EARLY IN LIFE WE WILL BE BETTER INDIVIDUALS, BETTER MEMBERS OF FAMILIES, BETTER NEIGHBORS, AND BETTER DISCIPLES OF JESUS CHRIST, WHO HIMSELF LEARNED TO WORK AS A CARPENTER.
>
> NEAL A. MAXWELL, "FRIEND TO FRIEND: GOSPEL OF WORK," *FRIEND*, JUNE 1975

> I DO NOT BELIEVE PEOPLE CAN BE HAPPY UNLESS THEY HAVE WORK TO DO. . . . IF WE LEARN TO WORK EARLY IN LIFE WE WILL BE BETTER INDIVIDUALS, BETTER MEMBERS OF FAMILIES, BETTER NEIGHBORS, AND BETTER DISCIPLES OF JESUS CHRIST, WHO HIMSELF LEARNED TO WORK AS A CARPENTER.
>
> NEAL A. MAXWELL, "FRIEND TO FRIEND: GOSPEL OF WORK," *FRIEND*, JUNE 1975

# Chapter Fourteen

## LOSING OURSELVES IN THE SERVICE OF OTHERS

- - - - - - - - - - - - - - - - - - - - - - - - - - - - - - - - - -

### MUSIC

"A Poor Wayfaring Man of Grief," *Hymns*, no. 29.
"Because I Have Been Given Much," *Hymns*, no. 219.
"Have I Done Any Good?," *Hymns*, no. 223.
"Let Us Oft Speak Kind Words," *Hymns*, no. 232.
"Love One Another," *Hymns*, no. 308.
"As Sisters in Zion," *Hymns,* no. 309.

- - - - - - - - - - - - - - - - - - - - - - - - - - - - - - - - - -

### SUMMARY

How can you tell a true disciple of Jesus Christ? By the way she treats other people! One way we show the Lord how much we love Him is by serving His children—our brothers and sisters. When we feel God's love deep inside our soul, we feel a desire to reach outside ourselves and bless others. A true understanding of the gospel of Jesus Christ compels us to love and serve.

If we want to be like Christ, we need to do as Christ did: serve. The Savior ministered daily to the needs of those around Him. When we open our spiritual eyes, we will see many opportunities around us for Christlike service and love. Loving and serving our neighbor isn't always easy, but that great feeling you get afterward is evidence that you're doing exactly what the Savior would do!

The gospel of Jesus Christ can be summed up in one word: love. The Spirit of the Lord is gentle and kind and influences us to do good and to be good. We need to be patient with others as they learn and grow, and not look for their faults, just as we would hope they would do for us. When we show kindness inside and outside our home, hearts are softened and peace is given to a troubled world.

Charity is the pure love of Christ and the greatest of all virtues. Charity cannot be developed in the abstract; it requires clinical, hands-on experience. It is a process, not an event. The more we serve others, the more genuine our love will become for others.

Introduce the sisters in your Relief Society to several great websites they can visit with their families to choose service projects in their area where they can reach out to others in their community.

- www.volunteermatch.org
- www.idealist.org
- www.serve.gov
- www.volunteers.org
- www.nationalservice.gov

## QUOTES

🌺 "Kindness is the essence of greatness and the fundamental characteristic of the noblest men and women I have known. Kindness is a passport that opens doors and fashions friends. It softens hearts and molds relationships that can last lifetimes." (Joseph B. Wirthlin, "The Virtue of Kindness," *Ensign*, May 2005.)

🌺 "Kindness has many synonyms—love, service, charity. But I like the word *kindness* because it implies action. It seems like something you and I can do. Kindness can be shown in so many ways." (Betty Jo N. Jepsen, "Kindness—A Part of God's Plan," *Ensign*, November 1990.)

🌺 "We learn that charity, though often quantified as the action, is actually the state of the heart that prompts us to love one another." (Elaine L. Jack, "Strengthened in Charity," *Ensign*, November 1996.)

🌺 "Charity is not just a precept or a principle, nor is it just a word to describe actions or attitudes. Rather, it is an internal condition that must be developed and experienced in order to be understood." (C. Max Caldwell, "Love of Christ," *Ensign*, November 1992.)

🌺 "The more we serve our fellowmen in appropriate ways, the more substance there is to our souls." (Spencer W. Kimball, "President Kimball Speaks Out on Service to Others," *New Era*, March 1981.)

🔹 "When you get the Spirit of God, you feel full of kindness, charity, long-suffering, and you are willing all the day long to accord to every man that which you want yourself." (John Taylor, *Teachings of Presidents of the Church: John Taylor* [2001], 21.)

🔹 "I am convinced that true brotherly love is essential to our happiness and to world peace. . . . We need to show our love, beginning in the home and then widening our circle of love to encompass our ward members, our less active and nonmember neighbors, and also those who have passed beyond the veil." (Jack H. Goaslind Jr., "Reach Out to Our Father's Children," *Ensign*, May 1981.)

. . . . . . . . . . . . . . . . . . . . . . . . . . . . . . . . . . . . . .

## ART

Jesus Christ, no. 1
City of Zion Is Taken Up, no. 6
The Sermon on the Mount, no. 39
Christ Healing the Sick at Bethesda, no. 42
The Good Samaritan, no. 44
Jesus Washing the Apostles' Feet, no. 55
Jesus Carrying a Lost Lamb, no. 64
King Benjamin Addresses His People, no. 74
Jesus Healing the Nephites, no. 83
Jesus Blesses the Nephite Children, no. 84
The Foundation of the Relief Society, no. 98
Service, no. 115
Young Couple Going to the Temple, no. 120

. . . . . . . . . . . . . . . . . . . . . . . . . . . . . . . . . . . . . .

## VIDEOS

"Love One Another": www.lds.org/media-library/video/2010-02-04
    -love-one-another
"Gordon Hinckley: Lessons I Learned as a Boy": www.lds.org/media
    -library/video/2009-01-01-gordon-hinckley-lessons-i-learned-as-a-boy
"Love Thy Neighbor": www.youtube.com/watch?v=lq5IzDW4ufA
"Charity: An Example of the Believers": www.lds.org/media-library
    /video/2010-04-05-charity-an-example-of-the-believers
"We Believe In Doing Good to All Men: Service": www.lds.org/media
    -library/video/2010-12-04-we-believe-in-doing-good-to-all-men
    -service

"The Good Samaritan": www.lds.org/media-library/video/1998-05-01
-the-good-samaritan?category=feature-films
"David Andre Koch, Feed My Sheep": www.lds.org/media-library
/video/2012-03-06-david-andre-koch-feed-my-sheep
"Feed My Lambs": www.lds.org/media-library/video/2012-06-1880
-feed-my-lambs
"Being a More Christian Christian": www.lds.org/media-library/video
/2012-10-5010-elder-robert-d-hales
"Ye Have Done It unto Me": www.lds.org/media-library/video/2011
-10-068-ye-have-done-it-unto-me

## OBJECT LESSONS

❀ Make "Friendship Fudge" during the lesson by passing around a gallon-size bag of the fudge ingredients. To form the sweet treat, the sisters have to mix the ingredients together by squishing the bag. (Pass around a few bags filled with the ingredients if you have a large class.)

Recipe:
- 4 cups powdered sugar
- 3 ounces softened cream cheese
- 1/2 cup softened margarine
- 1/2 cup cocoa
- 1 teaspoon vanilla
- 1/2 cup chopped nuts

When the ingredients are mixed together, roll into a log, slice, and serve.

❀ Have a contest with prizes to see which of the sisters has the longest hair, longest fingernails, highest shoe heels, heaviest church bag, and so on. You can bring a scale and ruler to determine winners. Next, ask who has the most Christlike love. Discuss how to measure that quality. Can it be measured?

❀ Teach the sisters how to knit or crochet so that during your lesson they can begin making leper bandages to send to the Church's Humanitarian Center! You'll find numerous service opportunities for your Relief Society at www.ldsphilanthropies.org. The bandages and other humanitarian items can be sent to the following address:

LDS Philanthropies
1450 N. University Ave.
Provo, UT 84604
Telephone: (801) 356-5300
Website: www.ldsphilanthropies.org

⚜ While teaching your lesson, remove your jacket, belt, shoes, and unbutton some buttons on your sleeves without explaining why. (Be modest!) At the end, say, "You probably won't remember a word I said by the time you get home, but you will never forget what I did. Actions speak louder than words." We can talk about being Christlike, but when we serve we truly are Christlike.

⚜ Pass around a mirror and ask the sisters to look in it. Ask them when they focused on their own image if they were able to see anyone else? (No.) By serving others, we focus less on our own problems and challenges and gain an improved perspective.

## ARTICLES

Joseph B. Wirthlin, "The Virtue of Kindness," *Ensign*, May 2005.
Betty Jo N. Jepsen, "Kindness—A Part of God's Plan," *Ensign*, November 1990.
Milly Day, "Kindness, Goodwill, Generosity," *Ensign*, January 1998.
Susan Hainsworth, "If You Would Serve Them, Love Them," *Ensign*, March 1986.
C. Max Caldwell, "Love of Christ," *Ensign*, November 1992.
Elaine L. Jack, "Strengthened in Charity," *Ensign*, November 1996.
Gene R. Cook, "Charity: Perfect and Everlasting Love," *Ensign*, May 2002.
Bonnie D. Parkin, "Choosing Charity: That Good Part," *Ensign*, November 2003.
Henry B. Eyring, "Feeding His Lambs," *Ensign*, February 2008.
Derek A. Cuthbert, "The Spirituality of Service," *Ensign*, May 1990.
Jeffrey R. Holland, "'Charity Never Faileth': A Discussion on Relief Society," *Ensign*, March 2011.
V. Dallas Merrell, "A Vision of Service," *Ensign*, December 1996.
Spencer W. Kimball, "Small Acts of Service," *Ensign*, December. 1974.
Gene R. Cook, "Charity: Perfect and Everlasting Love," *Ensign*, May 2002.

Russell C. Taylor, "The Joy of Service," *Ensign*, November 1984.

## CHALLENGE

Talk to your Relief Society president, compassionate service coordinator, bishop, or another ward leader to see who in your ward you or your family can serve. Your service can be anonymous or not.

## DOCTRINAL MASTERY PASSAGES

- Mosiah 2:17
- Moroni 7:45
- Moses 7:18
- D&C 64:9–11

## *PREACH MY GOSPEL*

2, 8, 62, 87, 115, 118, 123–26, 168–69

## NOTES

_____

_____

_____

_____

_____

_____

_____

_____

_____

_____

_____

_____

_____

_____

_____

_____

We learn that charity, though often quantified as the action, is actually the state of the heart that prompts us to love one another.

Elaine L. Jack, "Strengthened in Charity," *Ensign,* November 1996

We learn that charity, though often quantified as the action, is actually the state of the heart that prompts us to love one another.

Elaine L. Jack, "Strengthened in Charity," *Ensign,* November 1996

# *Chapter Fifteen*

## THE HOLY PRIESTHOOD

. . . . . . . . . . . . . . . . . . . . . . . . . . . . . . . . . . .

### MUSIC

"The Priesthood Is Restored," *Children's Songbook*, no. 89.
"Ye Elders of Israel," *Hymns*, no. 319.
"The Priesthood of Our Lord," *Hymns*, no. 320.
"Come, All Ye Sons of God," *Hymns*, no. 322.
"Rise Up, O Men of God," *Hymns*, no. 323.
"See the Mighty Priesthood Gathered," *Hymns*, no. 325.

. . . . . . . . . . . . . . . . . . . . . . . . . . . . . . . . . . .

### SUMMARY

The priesthood is the power and authority of God given to righteous men to enable them to act in God's name for the salvation of the human family. Earthly ordinances such as baptism, confirmation, administration of the sacrament, and temple sealing ordinances need to be performed by the correct priesthood authority in order to be valid in the eyes of the Lord. The same power that Christ used to create the earth is given to worthy men who are living on the earth now.

When the Savior established His Church during His earthly ministry, He chose humble men to serve as His apostles. When He needed to restore His gospel in latter-days, He did it through a humble young boy. The Lord always looks for the humble in spirit to bear His priesthood and to lead His Church. Each of the twelve Apostles holds all of the priesthood keys on earth; however, only the president of the Church can exercise them in full on behalf of the Church. The united voice of those who hold the keys of the kingdom of God will always guide us to spiritual safety.

Good men and women of all religions are blessed, but without correct divine authority, they cannot receive saving ordinances and attain celestial glory. As women, we can inspire priesthood holders around us to honor their priesthood power and use it to bless others' lives.

· · · · · · · · · · · · · · · · · · · · · · · · · · · · · · · · · · · · · · ·

## QUOTES

🔸 "Priesthood is to be used for the benefit of the entire human family, for the upbuilding of men, women, and children alike. There is indeed no privileged class or sex within the true Church of Christ. . . . Men have their work to do and their powers to exercise for the benefit of all the members of the Church. . . . So with woman: Her special gifts are to be exercised for the benefit and uplift of the race." (Brigham Young quoted in John A. Widtsoe, *Priesthood and Church Government* [Salt Lake City: Deseret Book, 1954], 92–93.)

🔸 "The man holds the Priesthood, performs the priestly duties of the Church, but his wife enjoys with him every other privilege derived from the possession of the Priesthood. This is made clear, as an example, in the Temple service of the Church. The ordinances of the Temple are distinctly of Priesthood character, yet women have access to all of them, and the highest blessings of the Temple are conferred only upon a man and his wife jointly." (John A. Widtsoe, comp., *Priesthood and Church Government*, [Salt Lake City: Deseret Book, 1965], 83.)

🔸 "Caring for others is the very essence of priesthood responsibility. It is the power to bless, to heal, and to administer the saving ordinances of the gospel." (James E. Faust, "Power of the Priesthood," *Ensign*, May 1997.)

🔸 "When we consider how few men who have lived on earth have received the priesthood and how Jesus Christ has empowered those individuals to act in His name, we should feel deeply humble and profoundly grateful for the priesthood we hold." (Richard G. Scott, "Honor the Priesthood and Use It Well," *Ensign*, November 2008.)

🔸 "With [the priesthood], nothing is impossible in carrying forward the work of the kingdom of God. . . . It is the only power on the earth that reaches beyond the veil of death." (Gordon B. Hinckley, "Priesthood Restoration," *Ensign*, October 1988.)

## ART

Jacob Blessing His Sons, no. 12
Moses Gives Aaron the Priesthood, no. 15
Calling of the Fishermen, no. 37
Christ Ordaining the Apostles, no. 38
Jesus Raising Jairus's Daughter, no. 41
Jesus Washing the Apostles' Feet, no. 55
John the Baptist Conferring the Aaronic Priesthood, no. 93
Melchizedek Priesthood Restoration, no. 94
Young Man Being Baptized, no. 103
The Gift of the Holy Ghost, no. 105
Blessing the Sacrament, no. 107
Passing the Sacrament, no. 108
Missionaries: Elders, no. 109
Missionaries: Sisters, no. 110

## VIDEOS

"Blessings of the Priesthood": www.lds.org/media-library/video/2009-05-20-blessings-of-the-priesthood

"Elder Perry on Priesthood Part 1": www.lds.org/media-library/video/2011-09-41-elder-perry-on-priesthood-part-1?category=topics/priesthood

"Elder Perry on Priesthood Part 2": www.lds.org/media-library/video/topics/priesthood?lang=eng&start=13&end=24&order=default

"Elder Perry on Priesthood Part 3": www.lds.org/media-library/video/2011-01-39-elder-perry-on-priesthood-part-3

"Elder Perry on Priesthood Part 4": www.lds.org/media-library/video/2011-02-33-elder-perry-on-priesthood-part-4

"Restoration of the Priesthood": www.lds.org/media-library/video/2010-05-1130-restoration-of-the-priesthood

"Willing and Worthy to Serve": www.lds.org/media-library/video/2012-04-3060-president-thomas-s-monson

"Let Every Man Learn His Duty: Aaronic Priesthood": www.lds.org/media-library/video/2010-12-06-let-every-man-learn-his-duty-aaronic-priesthood

"Becoming a Priesthood Man: Priesthood Duty": www.lds.org/media-library/video/2010-12-08-becoming-a-priesthood-man-priesthood-duty

"Be Valiant in Courage, Strength, and Activity": www.lds.org/media
-library/video/2012-10-3020-bishop-gary-e-stevenson
"Priesthood and Priesthood Keys—We Are Brothers": www.lds.org
/media-library/video/2012-10-006-priesthood-and-priesthood
-keys-we-are-brothers

## OBJECT LESSONS

- Ask someone in the class to hold an umbrella and keep someone in the class dry from the pretend rain that is falling. Note that the umbrella only needs to be held by one person, but both people are kept dry from the rain. So it is with the priesthood; while men can hold the priesthood, it is meant to bless everyone and keep us all protected from the storms of earthly life.

- Show the class a gyroscope. It's not just a toy, but also a scientific instrument. To make it work, you start it spinning and pull the string. Even on small surfaces, the gyroscope will spin and stay upright. The gyroscope principle is used in a special type of compass used on a ship because the movement won't affect it. There are many things that can knock us off course in life, but if we follow the leadership of the priesthood, our direction will always be correct.

- Help the sisters memorize a part of the oath and covenant of the priesthood in Doctrine and Covenants 84. Try some of the memorizing techniques found at www.wikihow.com/Memorize.

- Invite someone from each priesthood quorum to share with the sisters what their responsibilities are in serving as a deacon, teacher, priest, elder, and high priest. You might also invite a stake patriarch or a member of the Seventy if they're available.

## ARTICLES

Thomas S. Monson, "Our Sacred Priesthood Trust," *Ensign*, May 2006.

Dallin H. Oaks, "Priesthood Blessings," *Ensign*, May 1987.

Thomas S. Monson, "The Priesthood—A Sacred Gift," *Ensign*, May 2015.

Richard G. Scott, "Honor the Priesthood and Use It Well," *Ensign*, November 2008.

James E. Faust, "A Royal Priesthood," *Ensign*, May 2006.

Thomas S. Monson, "True to Our Priesthood Trust," *Ensign*, November 2006.

Henry B. Eyring, "Faith and the Oath and Covenant of the Priesthood," *Ensign*, May 2008.

Thomas S. Monson, "The Priesthood—A Sacred Gift," *Ensign*, May 2007.

. . . . . . . . . . . . . . . . . . . . . . . . . . . . . . . . .

## CHALLENGE

Volunteer to drive a deacon to do his fast-offering route on the next fast Sunday.

. . . . . . . . . . . . . . . . . . . . . . . . . . . . . . . . .

## DOCTRINAL MASTERY PASSAGES

- Abraham 3:22–23
- Matthew 16:15–19
- Ephesians 4:11–14
- D&C 1:37–38

. . . . . . . . . . . . . . . . . . . . . . . . . . . . . . . . .

## PREACH MY GOSPEL

32, 37, 83–84, 218

. . . . . . . . . . . . . . . . . . . . . . . . . . . . . . . . .

## NOTES

_____

_____

_____

_____

_____

_____

_____

_____

_____

_____

_____

PRIESTHOOD IS TO BE
USED FOR THE BENEFIT OF
THE ENTIRE HUMAN FAMILY,
FOR THE UPBUILDING OF MEN, WOMEN,
AND CHILDREN ALIKE. THERE IS INDEED NO
PRIVILEGED CLASS OR SEX WITHIN THE TRUE
CHURCH OF CHRIST. . . . MEN HAVE THEIR
WORK TO DO AND THEIR POWERS TO EXERCISE
FOR THE BENEFIT OF ALL THE MEMBERS OF THE
CHURCH. . . . SO WITH WOMAN: HER SPECIAL
GIFTS ARE TO BE EXERCISED FOR THE BENEFIT
AND UPLIFT OF THE RACE.

Brigham Young quoted in John A. Widtsoe,
*Priesthood and Church Government*
(Salt Lake City: Deseret Book,
1954), 92–93

PRIESTHOOD IS TO BE
USED FOR THE BENEFIT OF
THE ENTIRE HUMAN FAMILY,
FOR THE UPBUILDING OF MEN, WOMEN,
AND CHILDREN ALIKE. THERE IS INDEED NO
PRIVILEGED CLASS OR SEX WITHIN THE TRUE
CHURCH OF CHRIST. . . . MEN HAVE THEIR
WORK TO DO AND THEIR POWERS TO EXERCISE
FOR THE BENEFIT OF ALL THE MEMBERS OF THE
CHURCH. . . . SO WITH WOMAN: HER SPECIAL
GIFTS ARE TO BE EXERCISED FOR THE BENEFIT
AND UPLIFT OF THE RACE.

Brigham Young quoted in John A. Widtsoe,
*Priesthood and Church Government*
(Salt Lake City: Deseret Book,
1954), 92–93

# *Chapter Sixteen*
# THE POWER OF
# THE BOOK OF MORMON

- - - - - - - - - - - - - - - - - -

## MUSIC

"Search, Ponder, and Pray," *Children's Songbook*, 109.
"Book of Mormon Stories," *Children's Songbook*, 118.
"The Books in the Book of Mormon," *Children's Songbook*, 119.
"As I Search the Holy Scriptures," *Hymns*, no. 277.
"From Homes of Saints Glad Songs Arise," *Hymns*, no. 297.

- - - - - - - - - - - - - - - - - -

## SUMMARY

We can find more comfort and wisdom in the Book of Mormon than we can in all other books that have been written. The Book of Mormon is a sacred record that contains the fulness of the gospel and testifies that Jesus Christ is the Redeemer of the world.

The law of witnesses was fulfilled by three men who gave testimony when they saw an angel and the gold plates while hearing God's voice, as well as eight other men who handled the plates. Each setting was different, but the witnesses from both experiences never doubted in their minds or hearts of the truths they beheld. Each of us can be a witness of the Book of Mormon too.

- - - - - - - - - - - - - - - - - -

## QUOTES

- "I told the brethren that the Book of Mormon was the most correct of any book on earth, and the keystone of our religion, and a man would get nearer to God by abiding by its precepts than by any other book." (Joseph Smith, *History of the Church of Jesus Christ of Latter-day Saints* [Salt Lake City: Deseret Book, 1978], 4:461.)

🌀 "Each of us, at some time in our lives, must discover the [Book of Mormon] for ourselves—and not just discover it once, but rediscover it again and again." (Spencer W. Kimball, "How Rare a Possession—the Scriptures!," *Ensign*, September 1976.)

🌀 "I knew it was true, as well as I knew that I could see with my eyes, or feel by the touch of my fingers, or be sensible of the demonstration of any sense." (Brigham Young, *Journal of Discourses* [1856], 3:91.)

🌀 "The Book of Mormon is truly a witness for Jesus Christ and his plan of salvation for mankind. It is a witness that Jesus Christ, through Joseph Smith . . . , has again established his work in our day. We invite all mankind to read it and learn for themselves its powerful message." (James A. Cullimore, "The Book of Mormon," *Ensign*, May 1976.)

## ART

Mormon Abridging the Plates, no. 73
Moroni Hides the Plates in the Hill Cumorah, no. 86
Joseph Smith Seeks Wisdom in the Bible, no. 89
Joseph Smith Translating the Book of Mormon, no. 92

## VIDEOS

"A Book with a Promise": www.lds.org/media-library/video/2009-03-11-a-book-with-a-promise
"Prepared for Our Day": www.lds.org/media-library/video/2012-08-3110-prepared-for-our-day
"Book of Mormon Testimonies": www.lds.org/media-library/video/2011-06-8-book-of-mormon-testimonies
"Another Testament of Jesus Christ—Richard": www.lds.org/media-library/video/2009-04-064-another-testament-of-jesus-christ-richard
"What Is the Book of Mormon? A 60-Second Overview": www.lds.org/media-library/video/2015-00-1010-what-is-the-book-of-mormon-a-60-second-overview

## OBJECT LESSONS

🌀 Show the class an old, rotten banana and ask for a volunteer to eat it. (No one will want to.) Ask the class why they didn't want it.

Now hold up a good banana and ask why anyone would choose to eat this one. Explain that our lives are like fruit; people can tell what kind of people we are by the fruit we produce. Matthew 7:20 says, "Wherefore by their fruits ye shall know them." Ask, "What kind of fruit do you want to produce?" The Book of Mormon is the fruit that evidences the truthfulness of Joseph Smith's testimony. You may be the only Book of Mormon that people will ever "read." Live your lives so that others can tell you're a disciple of Christ and will want to know more.

- Invite the sisters to write their testimonies of the Book of Mormon inside copies that the missionaries can give away to their investigators. Take a picture of the sister to include with her written testimony.

- Have the sisters draw pictures and quotes of the truthfulness of the Book of Mormon that could be turned into memes and uploaded to their Pinterest boards. They could create memes that spotlight how the Book of Mormon has blessed their lives.

## ARTICLES

Ezra Taft Benson, "The Book of Mormon is the Word of God," *Ensign*, January 1988.

Ezra Taft Benson, "The Book of Mormon and the Doctrine and Covenants," *Ensign*, May 1987.

Daniel C. Peterson, "Mounting Evidence for the Book of Mormon," *Ensign,* January 2000.

L. Tom Perry, "Give Heed Unto the Word of the Lord," *Ensign*, June 2000.

Russell M. Nelson, "A Testimony of the Book of Mormon," *Ensign*, November 1999.

Boyd K. Packer, "The Book of Mormon: Another Testament of Jesus Christ—Plain and Precious Things," *Ensign*, May 2005.

## CHALLENGE

Set a goal to read the Book of Mormon this year in your personal scripture study. Calculate how many pages a day you'll need to read to accomplish your objective. You can find all kinds of reading calendar apps to help you with your goal!

## DOCTRINAL MASTERY PASSAGES

- Moroni 10:4–5
- Isaiah 29:13–14
- Ezekiel 37:15–17
- 2 Thessalonians 2:1–3
- 2 Timothy 3:16–17
- James 1:5–6

. . . . . . . . . . . . . . . . . . . . . . . . . . . . . . . . . . . . . . . . .

## *PREACH MY GOSPEL*

7, 38–39, 103–4, 110–11, 103–14, 130

. . . . . . . . . . . . . . . . . . . . . . . . . . . . . . . . . . . . . . . . .

## NOTES

_____

_____

_____

_____

_____

_____

_____

_____

_____

_____

_____

_____

_____

_____

_____

_____

_____

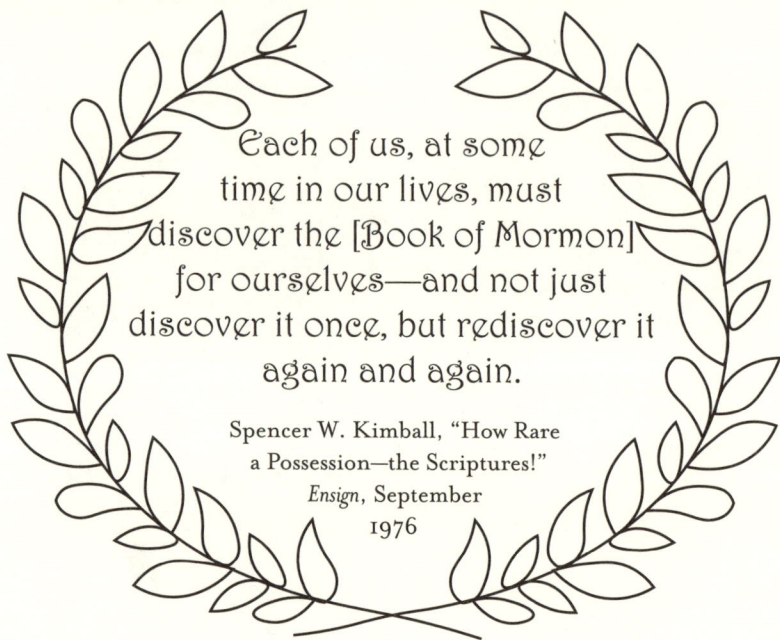

Each of us, at some
time in our lives, must
discover the [Book of Mormon]
for ourselves—and not just
discover it once, but rediscover it
again and again.

Spencer W. Kimball, "How Rare
a Possession—the Scriptures!"
*Ensign*, September
1976

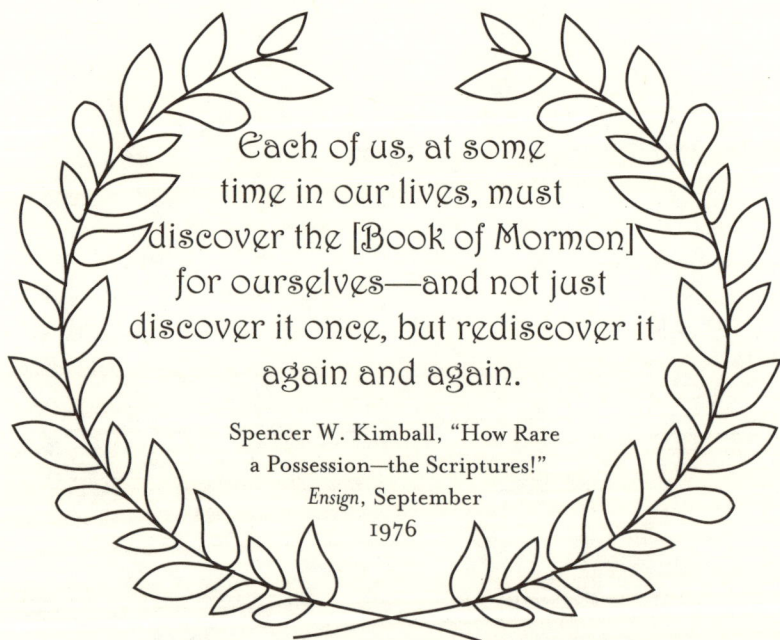

Each of us, at some
time in our lives, must
discover the [Book of Mormon]
for ourselves—and not just
discover it once, but rediscover it
again and again.

Spencer W. Kimball, "How Rare
a Possession—the Scriptures!"
*Ensign*, September
1976

# *Chapter Seventeen*
## CONTINUE IN THE GREAT PROCESS OF LEARNING

• • • • • • • • • • • • • • • • • • • • • • • • • • • • • • • • •

### MUSIC

"Welcome, Welcome, Sabbath Morning," *Hymns*, no. 280.
"We Listen to a Prophet's Voice," *Hymns*, no. 22.
"Teach Me to Walk in the Light," *Hymns*, no. 304.
"Thy Holy Word," *Hymns*, no. 279.

• • • • • • • • • • • • • • • • • • • • • • • • • • • • • • • • •

### SUMMARY

There are so many exciting things to learn! The more we know, the better we will be able to make wise choices, help our families, and contribute to society. The Lord has commanded us to educate our minds, hearts, and hands (see D&C 88:78–80). Education opens doors of opportunity and windows of blessings. Elder Russell M. Nelson wisely stated, "Education is the difference between *wishing* you could help other people and *being able* to help them" (Russell M. Nelson, "What Will You Choose?," *Ensign*, January 2015; emphasis in original).

What separates Mormons from other Christian churches is a *book*—the Book of Mormon. As we increase our education and learning, we should measure what we learn with the standards of gospel truth. We need to "school our spirits" even more. As members of the Church, we should be an ever-learning people—not just a learned people. It has been said that "When you educate a man you educate an individual; when you educate a woman you educate a whole family" (Dr. Charles D. McIver in *The Home Book of Quotations*, 8th ed., comp. Burton Stevenson [New York: Dodd, Mead and Co., 1956], 2193).

## QUOTES

🌸 "God desires that we learn and continue to learn, but this involves some unlearning. . . . The ultimate evil is the closing of the mind or steeling it against truth, resulting in the hardening of intellectual arteries." (Hugh B. Brown quoted in James E. Faust, "The Abundant Life," *Ensign*, November 1985.)

🌸 "Learning about sacred things should come first, providing a context and need for secular learning. If we want to return to our Heavenly Father's presence, our first priority should be to learn about his ways and his plan. The world would want to fool us into believing that there is insufficient time to engage in both spiritual and secular learning. I warn us not to be deceived by these philosophies of men. Our learning about sacred things will facilitate, even accelerate, our secular learning." (L. Tom Perry, "Learning to Serve," *Ensign*, August 1996.)

🌸 "There is much valuable reading you could do if you took a book with you to fill those islands of time . . . to learn in the moments we now waste. You could just have a book and paper and pencil with you. That will be enough. But you need determination to capture the leisure moments you now waste." (Henry B. Eyring, "Education for Real Life," *Ensign*, October 2002.)

🌸 "Faced with an excess of information in the marvelous resources we have been given, we must begin with focus or we are likely to become like those in the well-known prophecy about people in the last days—'ever learning, and never able to come to the knowledge of the truth' (2 Timothy 3:7). We also need quiet time and prayerful pondering as we seek to develop information into knowledge and mature knowledge into wisdom." (Dallin H. Oaks, "Focus and Priorities," *Ensign*, May 2001.)

## ART

Adam and Eve Teaching Their Children, no. 5
Isaiah Writes of Christ's Birth, no. 22
Boy Jesus in the Temple, no. 34
Mary and Martha, no. 45
Mormon Abridging the Plates, no. 73

King Benjamin Addresses His People, no. 74
Joseph Smith Seeks Wisdom in the Bible, no. 89

## VIDEOS

"Seek Learning": www.lds.org/media-library/video/2012-03-1020-seek
-learning

"Learning and Teaching in the Home and the Church—The Church":
www.lds.org/media-library/video/2014-06-002-learning-and
-teaching-in-the-home-and-the-church-the-church

"Elder and Sister Bednar—Secular and Spiritual Learning": www.lds
.org/media-library/video/topics/education

"Learning with Our Hearts": www.lds.org/media-library/video/2012
-10-1180-learning-with-our-hearts?category=standards-standards
/education-standards

"Standards: Education—The Glory of God Is Intelligence": www
.lds.org/media-library/video/2012-10-012-standards-education
-the-glory-of-god-is-intelligence?category=standards-standards
/education-standards

## OBJECT LESSONS

🔅 Invite several sisters to bring items to display that represent things
they're currently studying, and ask them to share a few things
they've learned with the class. Have them share how their learning
has blessed their lives and increased their faith.

🔅 Ask someone to lift various sizes of weights. Some weights should be
light and easy to lift and others should be heavy and quite difficult
to lift. Ask the sisters what they could do to help the sister without touching her weights. Inquire how building faith is like building
muscle. Talk about what kind of learning could be done to strengthen
faith. Ask how our faith can help us lift our heavy burdens in life.
Compare the lighter weights with leisure learning; contrast that with
the heavier weights that represent true study of topics.

🔅 Hand each person in class a clear marble and ask them to look
through it. The image of whatever they're looking at will be upside
down. Share Romans 12:2. In today's world where society calls good
evil and evil good, we can have faith that when Christ comes again
all will be transformed to that which is right. Having faith in Jesus

Christ helps us see correctly with our spiritual eyes. Having faith helps us to evaluate whether what we learn is truth or not.

• • • • • • • • • • • • • • • • • • • • • • • • • • • • • • • • • • •

## ARTICLES

David A. Bednar, "Learning to Love Learning," *Ensign*, February 2010.

Gordon B. Hinckley, "Words of the Prophet: Seek Learning," *New Era,* September 2007.

Dallin H. Oaks, "Learning and Latter-day Saints," *Ensign*, April 2009.

Mary N. Cook, "Seek Learning: You Have a Work to Do," *Ensign*, May 2012.

Thomas S. Monson, "To Learn, to Do, to Be," *Ensign*, November 2008.

Virginia H. Pearce, "The Ordinary Classroom—a Powerful Place for Steady and Continued Growth," *Ensign*, November 1996.

Aileen H. Clyde, "Charity and Learning," *Ensign*, November 1994.

Boyd K. Packer, "'To Be Learned Is Good If . . . ,'" *Ensign*, November 1992.

Dwan J. Young, "An Invitation to Grow," *Ensign*, May 1982.

Hartman Rector Jr., "Ignorance Is Expensive," *Ensign*, June 1971.

• • • • • • • • • • • • • • • • • • • • • • • • • • • • • • • • • • •

## CHALLENGE

Select a topic that you would like to learn more about and begin watching YouTube videos or reading articles about.

If you have never earned a college degree and would like to, consider the Pathway program offered online by BYU–Idaho. I am one of the college professors in Pathway and can promise that you will love it! Go to pathway.lds.org to learn more about how you can earn your degree online at a reduced cost and with other members of the Church from all over the world!

• • • • • • • • • • • • • • • • • • • • • • • • • • • • • • • • • • •

## DOCTRINAL MASTERY PASSAGES

- 2 Nephi 32:3
- 2 Nephi 32:8–9
- Mosiah 2:17
- Moroni 10:4–5
- Proverbs 3:5–6

- Isaiah 29:13–14
- John 7:17
- 2 Timothy 3:16–17
- D&C 89:18–21

# CHAPTER SEVENTEEN

## PREACH MY GOSPEL
3, 17–19, 22–25, 38, 89, 107, 119, 127, 171–73, 182

. . . . . . . . . . . . . . . . . . . . . . . . . . . . . . . . . . . . .

## NOTES

_____

_____

_____

_____

_____

_____

_____

_____

_____

_____

_____

_____

_____

_____

_____

_____

_____

_____

_____

_____

The ultimate evil is the closing of the mind or steeling it against truth, resulting in the hardening of intellectual arteries.

Hugh B. Brown quoted in James E. Faust, "The Abundant Life," *Ensign*, November 1985

The ultimate evil is the closing of the mind or steeling it against truth, resulting in the hardening of intellectual arteries.

Hugh B. Brown quoted in James E. Faust, "The Abundant Life," *Ensign*, November 1985

The ultimate evil is the closing of the mind or steeling it against truth, resulting in the hardening of intellectual arteries.

Hugh B. Brown quoted in James E. Faust, "The Abundant Life," *Ensign*, November 1985

# Chapter Eighteen

## VIRTUE—A CORNERSTONE ON WHICH TO BUILD OUR LIVES

### MUSIC

"Glorious Things Are Sung of Zion," *Hymns*, no. 48.
"Today, While the Sun Shines," *Hymns*, no. 229.
"Go, Ye Messengers of Glory," *Hymns*, no. 262.
"If You Could Hie to Kolob," *Hymns*, no. 284.

### SUMMARY

We only get one body; therefore, we must nurture and protect it. It houses our spirit and reveals our self-mastery and obedience. When we cling to virtue, our bodies and spirits glow with peace, happiness, and confidence before the Lord. We need to embrace all that is good and virtuous in the world so that there is no room in our lives for that which is evil and immoral.

We need to continually call upon the Lord for both mental and physical strength to resist the temptations and filth that the world offers. If we succumb to sin, we can be forgiven through sincere repentance and the Atonement of Jesus Christ.

### QUOTES

🌸 "You must be the guardians of virtue. . . . The Young Women values are Christlike attributes which include the value of virtue. We now call upon you to join with us in leading the world in a return to virtue. In order to do so, you 'must practise virtue and holiness' by eliminating from your life anything that is evil." (Elaine S. Dalton, "Love Her Mother," *Ensign*, November 2011.)

🕯 "Virtue consists, not in abstaining from vice, but in not desiring it." (George Bernard Shaw quoted in *And I Quote: The Definitive Collection of Quotes, Sayings, and Jokes for the Contemporary Speechmaker*, rev. ed. [Macmillan, 2003], 116.)

🕯 "I know of nothing that will qualify us for the constant companionship of the Holy Ghost as much as virtue." (Linda S. Reeves, "Worthy of Our Promised Blessings," *Ensign*, November 2015.)

🕯 "My earnest prayer is that you will have the courage required to refrain from judging others, the courage to be chaste and virtuous, and the courage to stand firm for truth and righteousness." (Thomas S. Monson, "May You Have Courage," *Ensign*, May 2009.)

🕯 "Now is the time for each of us to arise and unfurl a banner to the world calling for a return to virtue." (Elaine S. Dalton, "A Return to Virtue," *Ensign*, November 2008.)

## ART

Adam and Eve Kneeling at an Altar, no. 4
Adam and Eve Teaching Their Children, no. 5
City of Zion Is Taken Up, no. 6
Joseph Resists Potiphar's Wife, no. 11
Daniel Refusing the King's Food and Wine, no. 23
Mary and Martha, no. 45
Jesus Cleansing the Temple, no. 51
Jesus Washing the Apostles' Feet, no. 55
Mary and the Resurrected Jesus Christ, no. 59
Joseph Smith Seeks Wisdom in the Bible, no. 89
Young Couple Going to the Temple, no. 120

## VIDEOS

"A Return to Virtue": www.lds.org/general-conference/2008/10/a-return-to-virtue
"Virtue: For Such a Time as This": www.lds.org/media-library/video/2009-05-18-virtue-for-such-a-time-as-this
"Elder and Sister Bednar—Self-Esteem": www.lds.org/media-library/video/topics/virtue

"Virtuous Young Women": www.lds.org/media-library/video/2011-12
  -09-virtuous-young-women?category=standards-standards/dress
  -and-appearance-standards
"We Believe in Being Chaste": www.lds.org/media-library/video/topics
  /chastity
"195 Dresses": www.lds.org/media-library/video/standards-standards
  /dress-and-appearance-standards

## OBJECT LESSONS

- During the lesson, invite one of the sisters to *draw* your lesson on the chalkboard. In other words, she illustrates what she hears the class talk about. You can rotate other sisters as artists every five minutes. It's always fun and entertaining to see what they draw!

- Before the lesson, take pictures of as many sisters as you can who are participating in some kind of virtuous activity. Then during class, show all of the good things your Relief Society is doing in the community.

- Divide the class into small groups, and invite them to write a parable about something virtuous.

- Invite the young women to come in and share a message about virtue. It is one of the eight Young Women values emphasized in the Church.

## ARTICLES

Elaine S. Dalton, "A Return to Virtue," *Ensign*, October 2008.
Thomas S. Monson, "May You Have Courage," *Ensign*, May 2009.
Jeffrey R. Holland, "Personal Purity," *Ensign*, November 1998.
Neal A. Maxwell, "Reasons to Stay Pure," *New Era*, March 2003.
H. David Burton, "Let Virtue Garnish Your Thoughts," *Ensign*, November 2009.
Mary N. Cook, "A Virtuous Life—Step by Step," *Ensign*, May 2009.
D. Todd Christofferson, "Moral Discipline," *Ensign*, November 2009.

## CHALLENGE

Walk around your home and evaluate what is "virtuous, lovely, or of good report or praiseworthy," (Articles of Faith 1:13) and what is not.

Remove items and habits that draw you away from the spirit of the Lord. Do you have a picture of the temple or the Savior in your home? Are scriptures readily available on a bookshelf or nightstand? Can neighbors see that you believe in Christ when they walk into your home?

## DOCTRINAL MASTERY PASSAGES

- Mosiah 3:19
- Ether 12:27
- Moroni 7:45
- Moses 7:18
- Psalm 24:3–4
- 2 Timothy 3:16–17
- D&C 64:9–11
- D&C 89:18–21

## PREACH MY GOSPEL

77, 87, 90–91, 115, 118, 123–26, 168–69

## NOTES

_____

_____

_____

_____

_____

_____

_____

_____

_____

_____

_____

_____

_____

_____

_____

*Now* is the time for each of us to arise and unfurl a banner to the world calling for a return to virtue.

Elaine S. Dalton, "A Return to Virtue," *Ensign*, November 2008

*Now* is the time for each of us to arise and unfurl a banner to the world calling for a return to virtue.

Elaine S. Dalton, "A Return to Virtue," *Ensign*, November 2008

# *Chapter Nineteen*
## PRIESTHOOD LEADERSHIP IN THE CHURCH OF JESUS CHRIST

### MUSIC

"Behold! A Royal Army," *Hymns*, no. 251.
"Come, Listen to a Prophet's Voice," *Hymns*, no. 21.
"Come, Sing to the Lord," *Hymns*, no. 10.
"God Bless Our Prophet Dear," *Hymns*, no. 24.
"Praise to the Man," *Hymns*, no. 27.
"We Thank Thee, O God, for a Prophet," *Hymns*, no. 19.

### SUMMARY

God's "house" is a house of order. God communicates to His people through a living prophet, a man called through priesthood authority to represent Him. The prophet is also the President of the Church of Jesus Christ of Latter-day Saints, and he holds the keys of the kingdom on earth. The prophet receives revelation for the Church and leads the administration of priesthood ordinances.

The Lord also calls local priesthood leaders to preside and serve. When we sustain our priesthood leaders by the show of our raised hand in church, we are not voting for them; we are affirming our support and commitment to follow the Lord's anointed mouthpieces on earth.

### QUOTES

🏵 "Walk as leaders with the priesthood in the government of God. Walk with hands ready to help, with hearts full of love for your fellowmen. But walk with a toughness in righteousness." (Wendell J. Ashton, "Unchanging Principles of Leadership," *Ensign*, June 1971.)

🔹 "A prophet . . . is the authorized representative of the Lord. While the world may not recognize him, the important requirement is that God speaks through him." (A. Theodore Tuttle, "What Is a Living Prophet?," *Ensign*, July 1973.)

🔹 "Sustaining support of prophets, seers, and revelators is not in the upraised hand alone, but more so in our courage, testimony, and faith to listen to, heed, and follow them." (Dennis B. Neuenschwander, "Living Prophets, Seers, and Revelators," *Ensign*, November 2000.)

🔹 "When we sustain, it means we *do* something about our belief. Our testimony of the prophet turns into action when we sustain him." (Janette Hales Beckham, "Sustaining the Living Prophets," *Ensign*, May 1996.)

🔹 "Surely one of the crowning blessings of membership in this Church is the blessing of being led by living prophets of God." (Kevin R. Duncan, "Our Very Survival," *Ensign*, November 2010.)

## ART

Moses and the Brass Serpent, no. 16
Boy Samuel Called by the Lord, no. 18
Calling of the Fishermen, no. 37
Christ Ordaining the Apostles, no. 38
Jesus Washing the Apostles' Feet, no. 55
Jesus at the Door, no. 65
King Benjamin Addresses His People, no. 74
Abinadi before King Noah, no. 75
Alma Baptizes in the Waters of Mormon, no. 76
Captain Moroni Raises the Title of Liberty, no. 79
Two Thousand Young Warriors, no. 80
Samuel the Lamanite on the Wall, no. 81
Melchizedek Priesthood Restoration, no. 94
Elijah Appearing in the Kirtland Temple, no. 95
Latter-day Prophets, nos. 122–37

## VIDEOS

"Leading in the Savior's Way": www.lds.org/service/leadership
"Minister to Others": www.lds.org/service/leadership/minister-to-others

"Prepare Spiritually": www.lds.org/service/leadership/prepare-spiritually

"We Need Living Prophets": www.lds.org/media-library/video/2012
-04-15-we-need-living-prophets

"A Steady, Reassuring Voice": www.lds.org/media-library/video/2012
-08-3150-a-steady-reassuring-voice

"Follow the Prophet": www.lds.org/media-library/video/2015-01-006
-follow-the-prophet

## OBJECT LESSONS

- Gift wrap two boxes. Leave one empty and put some treats in the other one. Tell the class that one of the boxes has something special in it, while the other one has nothing. Ask a volunteer to choose a box. Let the volunteer see what's inside the box and ask the class if they want her to decide for them. Of course they'll say yes because she now knows what's in both boxes. We follow the prophet because he has "seen what's in the box" of life! He knows what choices we need to make in order to receive eternal rewards.

- Bring a beanbag that sisters will toss to other sisters during the lesson. Whoever has the beanbag will share one thing she is doing to sustain and support general and local priesthood leaders.

- Invite the sisters to sign a thank-you card for the prophet, the apostles, your bishop, or your stake president, thanking them for their priesthood leadership and service.

## ARTICLES

F. Michael Watson, "His Servants, the Prophets," *Ensign*, May 2009.

David B. Haight, "A Prophet Chosen of the Lord," *Ensign*, May 1986.

Jeffrey R. Holland, "'My Words . . . Never Cease,'" *Ensign*, May 2008.

Jeffrey R. Holland, "Prophets in the Land Again," *Ensign*, November 2006.

Dieter F. Uchtdorf, "Heeding the Voice of the Prophets," *Ensign*, July 2008.

Gordon B. Hinckley, "'We Thank Thee, O God, for a Prophet,'" *Ensign*, September 1991.

## CHALLENGE

Consider how you can help your husband, father, brother, or men in your ward to magnify their priesthood. How can you show Christlike leadership in your own service? Take cookies to your bishopric or home teachers to thank them for their priesthood service.

Read talks from the most recent General Conference to hear what our current prophet and apostles counseled us to do. Make a list of the things you need to work on in your life in order to say you are following the prophet 100 percent.

. . . . . . . . . . . . . . . . . . . . . . . . . . . . . . . . . . . . . . . . .

## DOCTRINAL MASTERY PASSAGES

- 1 Nephi 3:7
- Abraham 3:22–23
- Matthew 16:15–19
- Ephesians 4:11–14

. . . . . . . . . . . . . . . . . . . . . . . . . . . . . . . . . . . . . . . . .

## PREACH MY GOSPEL

7, 35–36, 44–45, 66, 75, 88

. . . . . . . . . . . . . . . . . . . . . . . . . . . . . . . . . . . . . . . . .

## NOTES

_____

_____

_____

_____

_____

_____

_____

_____

_____

_____

_____

WHEN WE
SUSTAIN, IT MEANS
WE DO SOMETHING
ABOUT OUR BELIEF. OUR
TESTIMONY OF THE PROPHET
TURNS INTO ACTION WHEN
WE SUSTAIN HIM.

JANETTE HALES BECKHAM,
"SUSTAINING THE LIVING PROPHETS,"
*ENSIGN*, MAY 1996

WHEN WE
SUSTAIN, IT MEANS
WE DO SOMETHING
ABOUT OUR BELIEF. OUR
TESTIMONY OF THE PROPHET
TURNS INTO ACTION WHEN
WE SUSTAIN HIM.

JANETTE HALES BECKHAM,
"SUSTAINING THE LIVING PROPHETS,"
*ENSIGN*, MAY 1996

WHEN WE
SUSTAIN, IT MEANS
WE DO SOMETHING
ABOUT OUR BELIEF. OUR
TESTIMONY OF THE PROPHET
TURNS INTO ACTION WHEN
WE SUSTAIN HIM.

JANETTE HALES BECKHAM,
"SUSTAINING THE LIVING PROPHETS,"
*ENSIGN*, MAY 1996

WHEN WE
SUSTAIN, IT MEANS
WE DO SOMETHING
ABOUT OUR BELIEF. OUR
TESTIMONY OF THE PROPHET
TURNS INTO ACTION WHEN
WE SUSTAIN HIM.

JANETTE HALES BECKHAM,
"SUSTAINING THE LIVING PROPHETS,"
*ENSIGN*, MAY 1996

# *Chapter Twenty*

## FELLOWSHIP WITH THOSE WHO ARE NOT OF OUR FAITH

### MUSIC

"Our Door Is Always Open," *Children's Songbook*, 254.
"O Lord of Hosts," *Hymns*, no. 178.
"We Are Sowing," *Hymns*, no. 216.
"Each Life That Touches Ours for Good," *Hymns*, no. 293.
"Love One Another," *Hymns*, no. 308.

### SUMMARY

The battle for religious freedom continues to be fought all over the globe. We need to link arms with all of the good men and women of this world to fight evil and help our fellowmen. There is so much good we can do together when we show love and respect for others not of our faith. How we treat others is evidence of our devotion to Jesus Christ.

Christians not of our faith created many of our favorite and most inspiring hymns including, "How Great Thou Art," "I Need Thee Every Hour," "I Stand All Amazed," "Because I Have Been Given Much," and "How Firm A Foundation." Let us praise God *together*, rather than allowing doctrinal differences to separate us.

### QUOTES

🌸 "I believe it would be good if we eliminated a couple of phrases from our vocabulary: 'nonmember' and 'non-Mormon.' Such phrases can be demeaning and even belittling. Personally, I don't consider myself to be a 'non-Catholic' or a 'non-Jew.' I am a Christian. I am a member of The Church of Jesus Christ of Latter-day Saints. That is how I prefer to be identified—for who and what I am, as opposed to being identified for what I am not. Let us extend that same courtesy to those who live among us. If a collective description is needed, then 'neighbors' seems to work well in most cases." (M. Russell Ballard, "Doctrine of Inclusion," *Ensign*, November 2001.)

🔹 "So often what people need so much is to be sheltered from the storms of life in the sanctuary of belonging." (Neal A. Maxwell quoted in Reed Stoddard, "As I Have Loved You" [Brigham Young University–Idaho devotional, April 18, 2006].)

🔹 "We are not the people of God when we are not united. Union is one of the fruits of the Spirit." ("Discourses and Writings of President George Q. Cannon," *Deseret Weekly*, June 26, 1897, 1.)

🔹 "I encourage you to build personal, meaningful relationships with your nonmember friends and acquaintances. Interest in the gospel may come later as a natural extension of a good friendship. Invitations to participate in gospel-related activities often will strengthen relationships with acquaintances. If they are not interested in the gospel, we should show unconditional love through acts of service and kindness, and never imply that we see an acquaintance only as a potential convert." (M. Russell Ballard, "The Hand of Fellowship," *Ensign*, November 1988.)

## ART

Ruth Gleaning in the Fields, no. 17
The Sermon on the Mount, no. 39
The Good Samaritan, no. 44
Go Ye Therefore, no. 61
Jesus Carrying a Lost Lamb, no. 64
Ammon Defends the Flocks of King Lamoni, no. 78
The Foundation of the Relief Society, no. 98

## VIDEOS

"Church Members should Extend Fellowship to All People, 1": www .lds.org/media-library/video/2012-08-2897-church-members -should-extend-fellowship-to-all-people-1
"Allison": www.lds.org/media-library/video/2011-01-030-allison

"Everyday Example: Religion in the Workplace": www.lds.org/media
   -library/video/topics/religious-freedom
"How Do I Love Thee?": www.lds.org/media-library/video/topics/love
"Anxiously Engaged: Acting in the Lord's Service": www.lds.org
   /media-library/video/2013-06-034-anxiously-engaged-acting-in
   -the-lords-service

## OBJECT LESSONS

Pass out M&M's, and ask the sisters how Christians are like M&M's. Some answers might include

1. The peanuts are sealed inside a delicious candy coating. Christians are sealed with the Holy Spirit.
2. Both Christians and M&M's come in a variety of personalities.
3. Both are filled with goodness.
4. Both are sweet.

Create a bingo board with blank squares. Invite the sisters to write words in each square that they think might be spoken during the lesson. (Tell them the title of the lesson if they don't know.) Whenever they hear you say one of the words on their bingo board, they get to cross it off or put a piece of candy on it. Whoever gets bingo first, wins a prize. You can continue playing during the lesson so several sisters can win. When we begin to love and care for our fellowmen, the Lord is surely shouting "bingo!" because we are finally getting it!

Invite the sisters to partner up and take turns talking nonstop for one minute each about organizations they are members of. Then, have them talk for another minute about what kind of positive influence they could have in those groups. Next, invite sisters to share with the class information about their organizations so that others can be more aware and possibly join in their good work.

## ARTICLES

M. Russell Ballard, "The Hand of Fellowship," *Ensign*, November 1988.
David B. Haight, "My Neighbor—My Brother!," *Ensign*, May 1987.
Carl B. Pratt, "Care for New Converts," *Ensign*, November 1997.

Ezra Taft Benson, "Our Commission to Take the Gospel to All the World," *Ensign*, May 1984.
James M. Paramore, "'They Taught and Did Minister One to Another,'" *Ensign*, May 1986.

## CHALLENGE

Look into joining an organization that seeks to do good in your area. Check out www.americanmothers.org—a wonderful organization dedicated to improving the lives of women and children. Talk with your bishop or stake president about creating an interfaith breakfast event where churches come together to celebrate the family. Talk to your ward or stake choir leaders about inviting neighboring churches to create an interfaith choir.

Consider creating a group at your school, work, or neighborhood to build each other up and accomplish good together. Talk about what some of the challenges are in your area and offer resources and ideas from your church that could be used to solve those problems.

## DOCTRINAL MASTERY PASSAGES

* Moses 7:18
* D&C 18:10, 15–16
* D&C 64:9–11

## PREACH MY GOSPEL

3, 8, 10–13, 19–21, 29, 31, 81–82, 84, 87, 107–8, 127, 138–39, 155–59, 167–70, 176, 183–87, 190–92, 195–99

## NOTES

_____

_____

_____

_____

_____

_____

I believe it would be good if we eliminated a couple of phrases from our vocabulary: "nonmember" and "non-Mormon." Such phrases can be demeaning and even belittling. Personally, I don't consider myself to be a "non-Catholic" or a "non-Jew." I am a Christian. I am a member of The Church of Jesus Christ of Latter-day Saints. That is how I prefer to be identified—for who and what I am, as opposed to being identified for what I am not. Let us extend that same courtesy to those who live among us. If a collective description is needed, then "neighbors" seems to work well in most cases.

M. Russell Ballard, "Doctrine of Inclusion,"
*Ensign*, November 2001

I believe it would be good if we eliminated a couple of phrases from our vocabulary: "nonmember" and "non-Mormon." Such phrases can be demeaning and even belittling. Personally, I don't consider myself to be a "non-Catholic" or a "non-Jew." I am a Christian. I am a member of The Church of Jesus Christ of Latter-day Saints. That is how I prefer to be identified—for who and what I am, as opposed to being identified for what I am not. Let us extend that same courtesy to those who live among us. If a collective description is needed, then "neighbors" seems to work well in most cases.

M. Russell Ballard, "Doctrine of Inclusion,"
*Ensign*, November 2001

# Chapter Twenty-One

# THE LATTER-DAY MIRACLE OF MISSIONARY WORK

## MUSIC

"I Want to Be a Missionary Now," *Children's Songbook*, 168.
"I Hope They Call Me on a Mission," *Children's Songbook*, 169.
"We'll Bring the World His Truth," *Children's Songbook*, 172.
"How Will They Know?," *Children's Songbook*, 182.
"Called to Serve," *Hymns*, no. 249.

## SUMMARY

There are many people in the world who are pure in heart, who would embrace the fulness of the gospel if they were given the opportunity. We have been given the knowledge of saving ordinances, as well as the divinely commissioned authority to provide those ordinances to the nations of the earth.

When we truly feel the Savior's love, we have the natural desire to extend it to those around us. When we do, our joy will be felt for eternity. The Lord entrusts us with this important work and it is our privilege to bring light to a dark world. Our righteous examples can illuminate our neighborhoods and draw the pure in heart to us.

When we help prepare young men and women to serve full-time missions and support them with prayers, food, finances, and referrals while they are laboring in the field, the Lord is pleased with our missionary efforts. As a result, we will have an even greater desire to open our mouths and bear our testimonies to a world that is seeking truth and direction. What a thrill it is to be a part of the exciting wave of missionary work happening right now as the Lord hastens His work!

In the spirit of love and kindness, our missionary work is about inviting people, not convincing them, to learn more. Rather than debate doctrine with nonbelievers, we gently love them and show them the Savior's love. The most important part of effective missionary work is not our carefully chosen words, but the Spirit with which we teach. This is the Lord's work and one of the most important things we can do here on earth.

## QUOTES

- "This isn't missionary work. This is missionary fun." (Neil L. Andersen, "It's a Miracle," *Ensign*, May 2013.)

- "We must develop love for people. Our hearts must go out to them in the pure love of the gospel, in a desire to lift them, to build them up, to point them to a higher, finer life that eventually will lead to exaltation in the celestial kingdom of God." (Ezra Taft Benson, "Keys to Successful Member-Missionary Work," *Ensign*, September 1990.)

- "For the Savior's mandate to share the gospel to become part of who we are, we need to make member missionary work a way of life." (Quentin L. Cook, "Be a Missionary All Your Life," *Ensign*, September 2008.)

- "It is impractical for us to expect that [full-time] missionaries alone can warn the millions in the world. Members must be finders. . . . If we are in tune, the Spirit of the Lord will speak to us and guide us to those with whom we should share the gospel. The Lord will help us if we will but listen." (Spencer W. Kimball quoted in Ezra Taft Benson, "President Kimball's Vision of Missionary Work," *Ensign*, July 1985.)

- "When we received the special blessing of knowledge of the gospel of Jesus Christ and took upon ourselves the name of Christ by entering the waters of baptism, we also accepted the obligation to share the gospel with others." (L. Tom Perry, "The Past Way of Facing the Future," *Ensign*, November 2009.)

- "The standard of truth has been erected; no unhallowed hand can stop the work from progressing; persecution may rage, mobs may combine, armies may assemble, calumny may defame, but the truth of God will go forth boldly, nobly, and independent, till it has penetrated every continent, visited every clime, swept every country, and sounded in every ear; till the purposes of God shall be accomplished, and the Great Jehovah shall say the work is done." (Joseph Smith Jr., "The Wentworth Letter," *Ensign*, July 2002.)

- "After all that has been said, the greatest and most important duty is, to preach the Gospel." (*Teachings of Presidents of the Church: Joseph Smith* [2007], 330.)

## ART

Esther, no. 21
Daniel Refusing the King's Food and Wine, no. 23
Boy Jesus in the Temple, no. 34
Calling of the Fishermen, no. 37
Mary and Martha, no. 45
Go Ye Therefore, no. 61
Abinadi before King Noah, no. 75
Alma Baptizes in the Waters of Mormon, no. 76
Ammon Defends the Flocks of King Lamoni, no. 78
Missionaries: Elders, no. 109
Missionaries: Sisters, no. 110

## VIDEOS

"The Work of Salvation": www.lds.org/media-library/video/hasten-the-work/special-broadcast-the-work-of-salvation

"The Church to Fill the Earth": www.lds.org/media-library/video/2010-07-059-the-church-to-fill-the-earth

"Developing the Faith to Find": www.lds.org/media-library/video/2007-04-024-developing-the-faith-to-find

"Loving and Serving Others": www.lds.org/media-library/video/2007-08-01-loving-and-serving-others

"The Opportunity of a Lifetime": www.lds.org/media-library/video/2011-10-3030-elder-w-christopher-waddell

"Why Mormons send missionaries around the world": www.lds.org/media-library/video/2010-05-1190-why-mormons-send-missionaries-around-the-world

# CHAPTER TWENTY-ONE

## OBJECT LESSONS

🌸 The spirit of missionary work will fill your classroom as you invite the sisters to share their conversion stories.

🌸 Set up a row of dominoes on the front table and then watch the chain reaction as you knock the first one down. Compare that to all of the lives that are touched for good by just one member of the Church being a good missionary.

🌸 Display a large basket of goodies on the table at the front of the class and begin to eat from it, expressing great delight. Ask the class to share why they love the gospel so much. Continue snacking and then explain that when we enjoy the blessings of the gospel without sharing it with others, it's like eating from a basket of goodies that you love and not sharing it with the class! Pass the basket around and invite everyone to join you in eating yummy treats. At the end of the lesson, ask the sisters how many of them didn't take a treat, ate it right away, or planned on saving it for later. Explain that doing missionary work is similar—even when we share the sweet gospel with others, some people will accept it and embrace it, others won't, and others might but not until after many years.

🌸 Invite the full-time missionaries to share some conversion stories and experiences with your class.

## ARTICLES

Earl C. Tingey, "Missionary Service," *Ensign*, May 1998.
Thomas S. Monson, "That All May Hear," *Ensign*, May 1995.
M. Russell Ballard, "Creating a Gospel-Sharing Home," *Ensign*, May 2006.
Dallin H. Oaks, "Sharing the Gospel," *Ensign*, November 2001.
Dallin H. Oaks, "The Role of Members in Conversion," *Ensign*, March 2003.
Ezra Taft Benson, "President Kimball's Vision of Missionary Work," *Ensign*, July 1985.

## CHALLENGE

Invite the full-time missionaries in your area over to dinner. Ask them about their investigators and find out what you can do to help.

Invite them to teach one of their investigators in your home or offer to go with them to teach.

* * * * * * * * * * * * * * * * * * * * * * * * * * * * * * * * * * * * * *

## DOCTRINAL MASTERY PASSAGES

- Moroni 10:4–5
- Isaiah 29:13–14
- Joseph Smith—History 1:15–20
- D&C 18:10, 15–16

* * * * * * * * * * * * * * * * * * * * * * * * * * * * * * * * * * * * * *

## *PREACH MY GOSPEL*

1–2, 4–5, 8–13, 19–21, 44–45, 81, 105, 107–8, 127, 138–39, 155–58, 174–76, 182–87, 190–92, 195–99, 203

* * * * * * * * * * * * * * * * * * * * * * * * * * * * * * * * * * * * * *

## NOTES

_____

_____

_____

_____

_____

_____

_____

_____

_____

_____

_____

_____

_____

_____

_____

_____

This isn't
missionary
work.
This is missionary
fun.
Neil L. Andersen, "It's
a Miracle," Ensign,
May 2013

This isn't
missionary
work.
This is missionary
fun.
Neil L. Andersen, "It's
a Miracle," Ensign,
May 2013

# Chapter Twenty-Two

## REACHING OUT WITH LOVE TO NEW CONVERTS AND LESS-ACTIVE MEMBERS

### MUSIC

"The Holy Ghost," *Children's Songbook*, 105.
"The Still Small Voice," *Children's Songbook*, 106.
"Come, All Ye Saints of Zion," *Hymns*, no. 38.
"The Lord Is My Shepherd," *Hymns*, no. 108.
"Dear to the Heart of the Shepherd," *Hymns*, no. 221.
"Come, All Whose Souls Are Lighted," *Hymns*, no. 268.

### SUMMARY

The parable of the lost sheep teaches us about the Savior's love for the one. It is a sacred duty and honor to help the Lord feed His sheep and find those who are lost. With kindness and patience, we can befriend those who are less active in the Church and help them feel the joy they once felt when they first joined the Church.

With the companionship of the Holy Ghost, we can receive inspiration about what to say and how to invite less-active members back into the fold. The goal is to help them remember the sacred covenants they made at baptism and to gain a desire to participate in additional ordinances that will bless their lives. The Holy Ghost has been given to us by a loving Heavenly Father to provide comfort, guidance, and a witness for truth.

## QUOTES

🐑 "Come back to the serenity that distills from the decision to live the commandments of your Elder Brother, Jesus the Christ." (Richard G. Scott, "We Love You—Please Come Back," *Ensign*, May 1986.)

🐑 "Love engenders faith in Christ's plan of happiness, provides courage to begin the process of repentance, strengthens the resolve to be obedient to His teachings, and opens the door of service, welcoming in the feelings of self-worth and of being loved and needed." (Richard G. Scott, "We Love You—Please Come Back," *Ensign*, May 1986.)

🐑 "Jesus said, 'Feed my sheep.' (John 21:16.) You can't feed them if you don't know where they are. You can't feed them if you give them reason to resist you. . . . The best foods with which to feed His sheep are charity and the restoration of dignity. By our actions we show our love." (Marvin J. Ashton, "'Give with Wisdom That They May Receive with Dignity,'" *Ensign*, October 1981.)

🐑 "So often what people need so much is to be sheltered from the storms of life in the sanctuary of belonging." (Neal A. Maxwell quoted in Reed Stoddard, "As I Have Loved You" [Brigham Young University–Idaho devotional, April 18, 2006].)

## ART

Moses and the Brass Serpent, no. 16
Ruth Gleaning in the Fields, no. 17
Boy Samuel Called by the Lord, no. 18
The Sermon on the Mount, no. 39
The Good Samaritan, no. 44
Go Ye Therefore, no. 61
Jesus Carrying a Lost Lamb, no. 64
Jesus at the Door, no. 65
The Foundation of the Relief Society, no. 98
Service, no. 115

## VIDEOS

"Feed My Sheep": www.lds.org/media-library/video/2014-01-025-feed-my-sheep

"Jesus Declares the Parable of the Lost Sheep": www.lds.org/media
-library/video/2011-10-063-jesus-declares-the-parable-of-the-lost-sheep

"Ye Have Done it Unto Me": www.lds.org/media-library/video
/2011-10-068-ye-have-done-it-unto-me

"The Good Shepherd": www.lds.org/media-library/video/2013-10
-1550-the-good-shepherd

"Waiting for the Prodigal": www.lds.org/media-library/video/2015-04
-4050-elder-brent-h-nielson

## OBJECT LESSONS

- Because this lesson will be given during the Christmas season, consider sharing some Christmas stories, singing carols, or making a simple ornament while discussing the life of Jesus Christ.

- Pass around a notebook that travels from sister to sister during the lesson. Invite the sisters to each write one sentence that would be an effective way to begin a conversation with a less-active member. Read their entries at the end of the class.

- Create a video presentation that includes photos of the sisters in your ward/branch so everyone can be familiar with each other. Take pictures of all the sisters to put on a wall in your Relief Society room.

- Play "Four Corners" so the sisters can get to know each other better. Give them a list of four things to choose from and assign a corner of the room to each one. Invite the sisters to stand in the corner that best represents their answer. Questions might include: What is your favorite season of the year? (Winter, spring, summer, or fall). Who is your favorite scripture hero? (Moses, Paul, Nephi, or Captain Moroni.) What is your favorite dessert? (Cheesecake, ice cream, anything chocolate, or pie.) Where is your favorite place to go on vacation? (Beaches, mountains, big cities, or staycations.) Which temple is your favorite? (Salt Lake, San Diego, the one closest to your home, or Nauvoo.)

## ARTICLES

Silvia H. Allred, "Feed My Sheep," *Ensign*, November 2007.

Ulisses Soares, "'Feed My Sheep,'" *Ensign*, November 2005.

Joseph B. Wirthlin, "Restoring the Lost Sheep," *Ensign*, May 1984.

# CHAPTER TWENTY-TWO

James E. Faust, "Dear Are the Sheep That Have Wandered," *Ensign*, May 2003.

Gordon B. Hinckley, "Find the Lambs, Feed the Sheep," *Ensign*, May 1999.

Robert D. Hales, "'When Thou Art Converted, Strengthen Thy Brethren,'" *Ensign*, May 1997.

## CHALLENGE

Look at your visiting teaching route to see if you can step it up a notch if you have less-active sisters on your list. Ask the Relief Society president if there is a sister or two in the ward who needs a new friend. Be that friend! Sit next to someone who is alone at church next week and introduce yourself.

## DOCTRINAL MASTERY PASSAGES

- 2 Nephi 32:3
- Moroni 10:4–5
- James 1:5–6
- D&C 8:2–3
- D&C 130:22–23

## *PREACH MY GOSPEL*

3, 18, 65, 89–93, 96–102

## NOTES

_____

_____

_____

_____

_____

_____

_____

_____

_____

{ SO OFTEN WHAT PEOPLE NEED SO MUCH IS TO BE SHELTERED FROM THE STORMS OF LIFE IN THE SANCTUARY OF BELONGING. }

NEAL A. MAXWELL QUOTED IN REED STODDARD, "AS I HAVE LOVED YOU" (BRIGHAM YOUNG UNIVERSITY—IDAHO DEVOTIONAL, APRIL 18, 2006)

{ SO OFTEN WHAT PEOPLE NEED SO MUCH IS TO BE SHELTERED FROM THE STORMS OF LIFE IN THE SANCTUARY OF BELONGING. }

NEAL A. MAXWELL QUOTED IN REED STODDARD, "AS I HAVE LOVED YOU" (BRIGHAM YOUNG UNIVERSITY—IDAHO DEVOTIONAL, APRIL 18, 2006)

# Chapter Twenty-Three
## THE BLESSINGS OF THE HOLY TEMPLE

### MUSIC

"High on the Mountain Top," *Hymns*, no. 5.
"God Is in His Holy Temple," *Hymns*, no. 132.
"We Love Thy House, O God," *Hymns*, no. 247.
"How Beautiful Thy Temples, Lord," *Hymns*, no. 288.
"Holy Temples on Mount Zion," *Hymns*, no. 289.

### SUMMARY

Sacred temples are built as schools for the Saints to receive eternal ordinances, make important covenants, and gain vital knowledge that will bind their families together forever and allow them to enter into the celestial kingdom. Attending the temple is a symbol of our faithful membership in the Church. Prophets have encouraged us to get a temple recommend and use it as often as we can. Being "temple worthy," even when we don't live near a temple, will allow us to become more like the Savior in thought and deed.

### QUOTES

- "I think there is no place in the world where I feel closer to the Lord than in one of His holy temples." (Thomas S. Monson, "Blessings of the Temple," *Ensign*, October 2010.)

- "It is a place of peace, solitude, and inspiration. Regular attendance will enrich your life with greater purpose. It will permit you to provide deceased ancestors the exalting ordinances you have received.

Go to the temple. You know it is the right thing to do. Do it now." (Richard G. Scott, "Receive the Blessings of the Temple," *Ensign*, May 1999.)

🔹 "The Lord's work is one majestic work focused upon hearts, covenants, and priesthood ordinances." (David A. Bednar, "Missionary, Family History, and Temple Work," *Ensign*, October 2014.)

🔹 "Always prayerfully express gratitude for the incomparable blessings that flow from temple ordinances. Live each day so as to give evidence to Father in Heaven and His Beloved Son of how very much those blessings mean to you." (Richard G. Scott, "How Can We Make the Most of Temple Attendance?," *New Era*, March 2012.)

🔹 "When a temple is conveniently nearby, small things may interrupt your plans to go to the temple. Set specific goals, considering your circumstances, of when you can and will participate in temple ordinances. Then, do not allow anything to interfere with that plan. This pattern will guarantee that those who live in the shadow of a temple will be as blessed as are those who plan far ahead and make a long trip to the temple." (Richard G. Scott, "How Can We Make the Most of Temple Attendance?," *New Era*, March 2012.)

## ART

Jesus Christ, no. 1
Boy Jesus in the Temple, no. 34
Jesus Cleansing the Temple, no. 51
My Father's House, no. 52
Melchizedek Priesthood Restoration, no. 94
Elijah Appearing in the Kirtland Temple, no. 95
Kirtland Temple, no. 117
Nauvoo Illinois Temple, no. 118
Salt Lake Temple, no. 119
Young Couple Going to the Temple, no. 120
Temple Baptismal Font, no. 121

## VIDEOS

"To Have Peace and Happiness": www.lds.org/media-library/video
/2010-09-0040-to-have-peace-and-happiness

"Mormon Temples": www.lds.org/media-library/video/topics/temples

"Why Mormons Build Temples": www.lds.org/media-library/video
/2010-05-1210-why-mormons-build-temples

"Temples are a Beacon": www.lds.org/media-library/video/2012-01
-002-temples-are-a-beacon

"Endowed with Power": www.lds.org/media-library/video/2010-07
-126-endowed-with-power

"The Blessings of the Temple": www.lds.org/media-library/video/2009
-03-10-the-blessings-of-the-temple

## OBJECT LESSONS

- Show the class several items (or pictures of items): candy, coins, a twenty dollar bill, a stuffed animal, a diamond ring, and so on. Ask the class which items they think a baby would be most interested in. (The candy and stuffed animal.) Ask why the baby wouldn't select the most expensive item? (She doesn't understand the value of it.) Talk about how some people don't understand the value of temples, so they make choices that might prevent them from being worthy to enter the temple.

- Invite the sisters to share pictures of their favorite temple and share faith-promoting stories about how the temple has blessed their lives.

- Search the Internet as a class and find some of the newer temples that are under construction or being remodeled. Look at them via Google Earth and Street View!

- Invite someone in your ward who has recently attended the temple for the first time to talk about how they prepared and how their experience made them feel closer to the Savior. You can also invite some of the youth to share their experiences about going to the temple to do baptisms for the dead.

## ARTICLES

Russell M. Nelson, "Prepare for Blessings of the Temple," *Ensign*, March 2002.

David E. Sorensen, "The Doctrine of Temple Work," *Ensign*, October 2003.

Howard W. Hunter, "We Have a Work to Do," *Ensign*, March 1995.

Richard G. Scott, "Receive the Temple Blessings," *Ensign*, May 1999.

Howard W. Hunter, "A Temple-Motivated People," *Ensign*, February 1995.

Stacy Vickery, "Temple Blessing Now and Eternally," *Ensign*, September 2011.

Dennis B. Neuenschwander, "Bridges and Eternal Keepsakes," *Ensign*, May 1999.

• • • • • • • • • • • • • • • • • • • • • • • • • • • • • • • •

## CHALLENGE

Hang a picture of the temple in your home. Attend the temple preparation class if your ward/branch offers one. Renew your temple recommend (if it has expired) and keep it in your wallet. Choose your next family's vacation destination based on which temple you would like to visit!

• • • • • • • • • • • • • • • • • • • • • • • • • • • • • • • •

## DOCTRINAL MASTERY PASSAGES

• 1 Corinthians 15:20–22      • D&C 131:1–4

• • • • • • • • • • • • • • • • • • • • • • • • • • • • • • • •

## *PREACH MY GOSPEL*

31–32, 47–50, 52–54, 85–86, 159–65

• • • • • • • • • • • • • • • • • • • • • • • • • • • • • • • •

## NOTES

_____

_____

_____

_____

_____

_____

_____

_____

_____

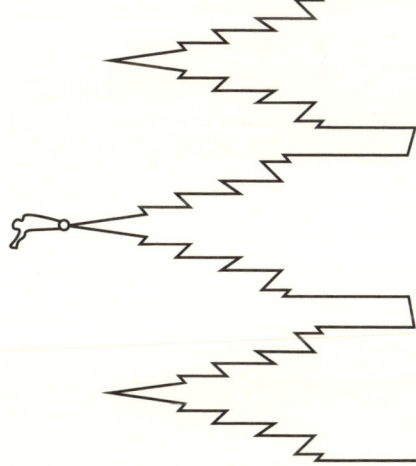

*I think there is no place in the world where I feel closer to the Lord than in one of His holy temples.*

Thomas S. Monson, "Blessings of the Temple," *Ensign*, October 2010

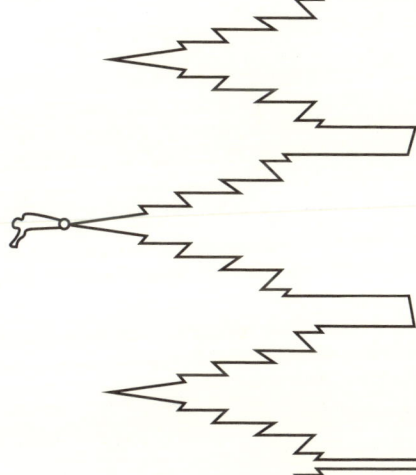

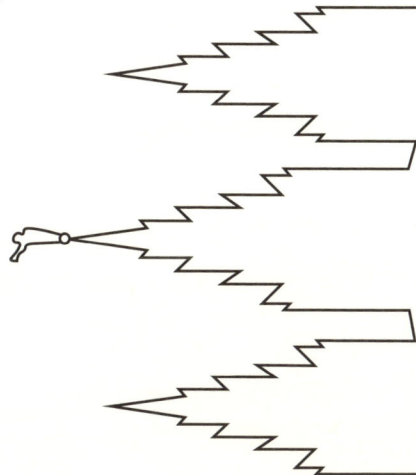

*I think there is no place in the world where I feel closer to the Lord than in one of His holy temples.*

Thomas S. Monson, "Blessings of the Temple," *Ensign*, October 2010

*I think there is no place in the world where I feel closer to the Lord than in one of His holy temples.*

Thomas S. Monson, "Blessings of the Temple," *Ensign*, October 2010

# Chapter Twenty-Four

## THE ATONEMENT OF JESUS CHRIST—VAST IN ITS REACH, INTIMATE IN ITS EFFECT

### MUSIC

"Our Savior's Love," *Hymns*, no. 113.
"I Believe in Christ," *Hymns*, no. 134.
"In Humility, Our Savior," *Hymns*, no. 172.
"God Loved Us, So He Sent His Son," *Hymns*, no. 187.
"Behold the Great Redeemer Die," *Hymns*, no. 191.
"Christ the Lord Is Risen Today," *Hymns*, no. 200.

### SUMMARY

Jesus Christ was chosen and foreordained to come to earth to atone for our sins and teach us how to return to our Heavenly Father. Jesus Christ was not just a good man, effective teacher, or inspiring leader, but the Redeemer of the world. As members of the Church, we not only believe that the Savior lived on this earth and died for our sins, but that He still lives! Our lives should reflect those beliefs. Our actions should testify to all that we know He will soon come again.

Our understanding of the divine mission of Jesus Christ should compel us to act—to show greater love and kindness and to share His gospel with others. The gospel is more than good news—it's *great* news! We should live our lives so that there will be absolutely no question that Mormons are Christians. Feasting daily on the scriptures and praying sincerely will fill us with hope, joy, and a powerful testimony. By following Jesus Christ we can find joy in this life and in the next.

## QUOTES

- "I weep for joy when I contemplate the significance of it all. To be redeemed is to be atoned—received in the close embrace of God with an expression not only of His forgiveness, but of our oneness of heart and mind." (Russell M. Nelson, "The Atonement," *Ensign*, November 1996.)

- "The Redeemer loves you and will help you do the essential things that bring happiness now and forever." (Richard G. Scott, "Jesus Christ, Our Redeemer," *Ensign*, May 1997.)

- "Ever and always [the Atonement] offers amnesty from transgression and from death if we will but repent. . . . Repentance is the key with which we can unlock the prison from inside . . . and agency is ours to use it." (Boyd K. Packer, "Atonement, Agency, Accountability," *Ensign*, May 1988.)

- "[The Lord's] atonement is the most transcendent event that ever has or ever will occur from Creation's dawn through all the ages of a never-ending eternity." (Bruce R. McConkie, "The Purifying Power of Gethsemane," *Ensign*, May 1985.)

- "The Savior's birth, ministry, atoning sacrifice, Resurrection, and promised coming all bear witness to His divinity." (Ezra Taft Benson, "Five Marks of the Divinity of Jesus Christ," *Ensign*, December 2001.)

## ART

Isaiah Writes of Christ's Birth, no. 22
The Birth of Jesus, no. 30
Boy Jesus in the Temple, no. 34
John the Baptist Baptizing Jesus, no. 35
Triumphal Entry, no. 50
Jesus Praying in Gethsemane, no. 56
The Crucifixion, no. 57
Burial of Jesus, no. 58
Mary and the Resurrected Jesus Christ, no. 59
Jesus Shows His Wounds, no. 60
The Ascension of Jesus, no. 62
The Second Coming, no. 66
Jesus Teaching in the Western Hemisphere, no. 82

## VIDEOS

"Jesus Christ Suffered for us": www.lds.org/media-library/video/2010
-05-1150-jesus-christ-suffered-for-us

"'He Is Not Here: for He Is Risen'": www.lds.org/media-library/video
/2013-10-1210-he-is-not-here-for-he-is-risen

"The Mediator": www.lds.org/media-library/video/the-mediator

"To This End Was I Born": www.lds.org/media-library/video/2014-01
-007-to-this-end-was-i-born?lang=eng&_r=1

"Lifting Burdens: The Atonement of Jesus Christ": www.youtube.com
/watch?v=coef8G5ax6E

. . . . . . . . . . . . . . . . . . . . . . . . . . . . . . . . . . . . . . .

## OBJECT LESSONS

Show the class some different kinds of keys: old-fashioned ones, key rings, hotel card keys, and so on. Explain how the keys allow you to enter appealing locations such as fancy hotel rooms, luxury vehicles, and bank safes. Some people judge their lives by the keys they possess: an education is the key to a good career; a car is a key to freedom; a good job is the key to power and wealth; a key to a large home represents success and security. But there is only one key that opens the most important destination of all—Jesus Christ is the key to eternal life with our Father in Heaven.

Ask someone to draw a picture of something complicated. Now give them a pattern to trace. Jesus is our pattern to show us how to create our lives here on earth so that we can live an eternal life with Heavenly Father.

Invite a volunteer to build a structure with building blocks on her lap. Ask the sisters sitting next to her to jiggle her shoulders or legs. Her structure will most likely fall. Now ask her to build one on top of a table at the front of the room. Invite some sisters to try to jiggle her again. This time, her structure won't fall because it has the stability of the table. Our testimonies need to be built on the Atonement of the Savior. That is the solid foundation that will prevent our testimonies and lives from falling apart.

. . . . . . . . . . . . . . . . . . . . . . . . . . . . . . . . . . . . . . .

## ARTICLES

Kent F. Richards, "The Atonement Covers All Pain," *Ensign*, May 2011.

Cecil O. Samuelson Jr., "What Does the Atonement Mean to You?," *Ensign*, April 2009.

Marion G. Romney, "Christ's Atonement: The Gift Supreme," *Ensign*, December 1973.

James E. Faust, "The Atonement: Our Greatest Hope," *Ensign*, November 2001.

Dallin H. Oaks, "Strengthened by the Atonement of Jesus Christ," *Ensign*, November 2015.

M. Russell Ballard, "The Atonement and the Value of One Soul," *Ensign*, May 2004.

## CHALLENGE

Write your testimony of the Savior and how you feel about the Atonement. Share your testimony with your family, someone serving a full-time mission, or a nonmember. Like Nephi's "small plates," begin a spiritual journal where you write about faith-building experiences you are having in your life. This will be a source of inspiration for your posterity.

## DOCTRINAL MASTERY PASSAGES

- Helaman 5:12
- 3 Nephi 27:27
- Genesis 1:26–27
- Isaiah 53:3–5
- Matthew 16:15–19
- Luke 24:36–39
- John 3:5
- John 17:3
- 1 Corinthians 15:20–22
- D&C 19:16–19
- D&C 76:22–24
- D&C 130:22–23

## *PREACH MY GOSPEL*

34, 37, 47–48, 51–52, 60–61, 90, 105, 116, 123–26

## NOTES

_____

_____

_____

_____

THE REDEEMER LOVES YOU
AND WILL HELP YOU DO
THE ESSENTIAL THINGS
THAT BRING HAPPINESS
NOW AND FOREVER.

RICHARD G. SCOTT, "JESUS CHRIST,
OUR REDEEMER," *ENSIGN*, MAY 1997

THE REDEEMER LOVES YOU
AND WILL HELP YOU DO
THE ESSENTIAL THINGS
THAT BRING HAPPINESS
NOW AND FOREVER.

RICHARD G. SCOTT, "JESUS CHRIST,
OUR REDEEMER," *ENSIGN*, MAY 1997

# Chapter Twenty-Five
## MOVE FORWARD WITH FAITH

. . . . . . . . . . . . . . . . . . . . . . . . . . . . . .

### MUSIC

"Faith of Our Fathers," *Hymns*, no. 84.
"Come unto Him," *Hymns*, no. 114.
"When Faith Endures," *Hymns*, no. 128.
"Testimony," *Hymns*, no. 137.
"True to the Faith," *Hymns*, no. 254.
"Go Forth with Faith," *Hymns*, no. 263.

. . . . . . . . . . . . . . . . . . . . . . . . . . . . . .

### SUMMARY

The first principle of the gospel isn't just faith, but faith in the Lord Jesus Christ. Faith is a belief in the Lord with our spiritual eyes even though we haven't seen Him with our physical eyes. It is a principle of action that compels us to pray, be obedient, and trust in His promises. We increase our faith by testing and studying His words. Faith has the power to move mountains, perform miracles, and prove us worthy to see God.

Our faith can provide the light we need to be able to live in a dark world. When doubts begin to enter our mind and heart, we need to hold onto the things we know to be true and the Lord will help us to build on that foundation.

. . . . . . . . . . . . . . . . . . . . . . . . . . . . . .

### QUOTES

🌸 "Faith in Jesus Christ takes us beyond mere acceptance of the Savior's identity and existence. It includes having complete confidence in His infinite and eternal redemptive power." (James O. Mason, "Faith in Jesus Christ," *Ensign*, April 2001.)

- "Spiritual light rarely comes to those who merely sit in darkness waiting for someone to flip a switch. It takes an act of faith to open our eyes to the Light of Christ. Spiritual light cannot be discerned by carnal eyes." (Dieter F. Uchtdorf, "The Hope of God's Light," *Ensign*, May 2013.)

- "Faith is not only a feeling; it is a decision." (Neil L. Andersen, "You Know Enough," *Ensign*, November 2008.)

- "Only faith in the Lord Jesus Christ and His Atonement can bring us peace, hope, and understanding." (Robert D. Hales, "Finding Faith in the Lord Jesus Christ," *Ensign*, November 2004.)

- "We promote the process of strengthening our faith when we do what is right—increased faith always follows." (L. Whitney Clayton, "'Help Thou Mine Unbelief,'" *Ensign*, November 2001.)

- "Faith in the Lord Jesus Christ is a conviction and trust that God knows us and loves us and will hear our prayers and answer them with what is best for us." (Dallin H. Oaks, "'Faith in the Lord Jesus Christ,'" *Ensign*, May 1994.)

## ART

Building the Ark, no. 7
Abraham Taking Isaac to Be Sacrificed, no. 9
Moses and the Brass Serpent, no. 16
Esther, no. 21
Three Men in the Fiery Furnace, no. 25
Daniel in the Lions' Den, no. 26
Jesus Calms the Storm, no. 40
Jesus Raising Jairus's Daughter, no. 41
Christ Walking on the Water, no. 43
Christ and the Children, no. 47
Jesus Shows His Wounds, no. 60
The Liahona, no. 68
Lehi and His People Arrive in the Promised Land, no. 71
Enos Praying, no. 72
Abinadi before King Noah, no. 75
Alma Baptizes in the Waters of Mormon, no. 76
Two Thousand Young Warriors, no. 80

The Brother of Jared Sees the Finger of the Lord, no. 85
Joseph Smith Seeks Wisdom in the Bible, no. 89
The First Vision, no. 90
Mary Fielding Smith and Joseph F. Smith Crossing the Plains, no. 101
Young Man Being Baptized, no. 103
Girl Being Baptized, no. 104
Christ and Children from around the World, no. 116

## VIDEOS

"By Faith": www.lds.org/media-library/video/2016-03-018-by-faith

"Dana's Testimony": www.lds.org/media-library/video/missionary/our
-faith

"By Faith All Things Are Fulfilled": www.lds.org/media-library/video
/topics/faith

"Light Switch": www.lds.org/media-library/video/2015-06-023-light
-switch?category=topics/faith

"Faith and Works": www.lds.org/media-library/video/2012-06-2060
-faith-and-works?category=topics/faith

"Faith and Trials": www.lds.org/media-library/video/2011-03-086
-faith-and-trials?category=topics/faith

"A Test of Faith": www.lds.org/media-library/video/2012-06-1240-a
-test-of-faith?category=topics/faith

## OBJECT LESSONS

Invite the class to sing "I Am a Child of God," and then tell them the story behind the words. Originally the words read "Teach me all that I must *know* to live with Him someday," but President Spencer W. Kimball said that knowing is not enough—we have to *do*. A leader doesn't just tell other people what to do, but is willing to do them herself as well. Show people; don't just tell people.

Ask for a brave volunteer who is willing to be blindfolded and show trust in you. Spin her around a few times and tell her walk to the door. Give her instructions every once in a while so it looks like she might run into something, but when she gets close, have her turn and avoid hitting into anything. (The class will be worried for her.) Finally, as she is walking toward the door, have someone place a chair in that spot. Tell her to sit down where the chair was placed—she won't expect a chair to be there. Have her take off the blindfold after she sits down and talk about what thoughts went through her mind. Talk about her doubts and the doubts of the sisters who watched, as well as why it is so important to put trust in someone who will never deceive us (the Lord).

Put clear vinegar in a clear glass so the sisters think it is filled with water. Ask the sisters to think very hard about what could be done to make the water overflow. Did their thoughts make any change? (No.) Add some baking soda and the vinegar will immediately begin to bubble up. In other words, we need to take action. When we act, our faith has more power.

## ARTICLES

Neil L. Andersen, "Faith Is Not by Chance, but by Choice," *Ensign*, November 2015.

Richard G. Scott, "Make the Exercise of Faith Your First Priority," *Ensign*, November 2014.

Russell M. Nelson, "Face the Future with Faith," *Ensign*, May 2011.

Russell M. Nelson, "Let Your Faith Show," *Ensign*, May 2014.

James E. Faust, "The Shield of Faith," *Ensign*, May 2000.

Gordon B. Hinckley, "Faith: The Essence of True Religion," *Ensign*, October 1995.

Russell M. Nelson, "Faith in Jesus Christ," *Ensign*, March 2008.

Kevin W. Pearson, "Faith in the Lord Jesus Christ," *Ensign*, May 2009.

Gordon B. Hinckley, "The Cornerstones of Our Faith," *Ensign*, November 1984.

Robert D. Hales, "Finding Faith in the Lord Jesus Christ," *Ensign*, November 2004.

Gordon B. Hinckley, "'Be Not Faithless,'" *Ensign*, April 1989.

Quentin L. Cook, "Live by Faith and Not by Fear," *Ensign*, November 2007.

## CHALLENGE

Write a list of all the gospel principles you *know* to be true and *how* you came to that knowledge and understanding.

## DOCTRINAL MASTERY PASSAGES

- 1 Nephi 3:7
- Ether 12:6
- Ether 12:27
- Moroni 7:45
- Moroni 10:4–5
- Proverbs 3:5–6

- Matthew 5:14–16
- Ephesians 4:11–14
- James 2:17–18
- Joseph Smith—History 1:15–20
- D&C 1:37–38

. . . . . . . . . . . . . . . . . . . . . . . . . . . . . . . . . . . .

## *PREACH MY GOSPEL*

18, 22, 38, 61, 90–102, 115–16, 155

. . . . . . . . . . . . . . . . . . . . . . . . . . . . . . . . . . . .

## NOTES

_____

_____

_____

_____

_____

_____

_____

_____

_____

_____

_____

_____

_____

_____

_____

SPIRITUAL LIGHT RARELY
COMES TO THOSE WHO MERELY
SIT IN DARKNESS WAITING FOR
SOMEONE TO FLIP A SWITCH. IT
TAKES AN ACT OF FAITH TO OPEN
OUR EYES TO THE LIGHT OF
CHRIST. SPIRITUAL LIGHT
CANNOT BE
DISCERNED BY
CARNAL
EYES.

DIETER F. UCHTDORF, "THE
HOPE OF GOD'S LIGHT,"
*ENSIGN*, MAY 2013

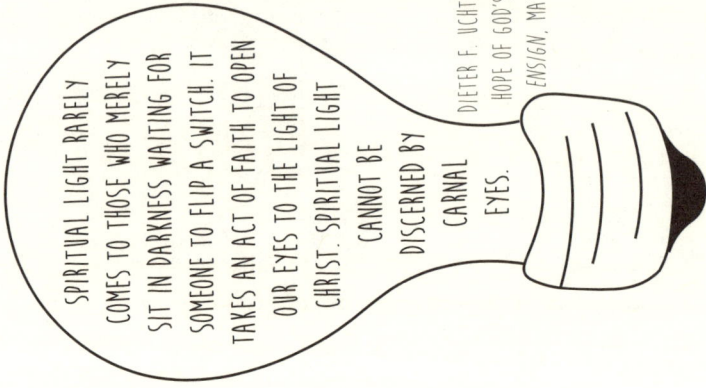

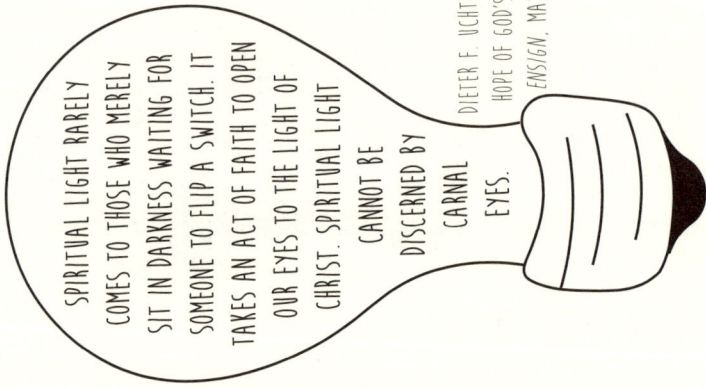

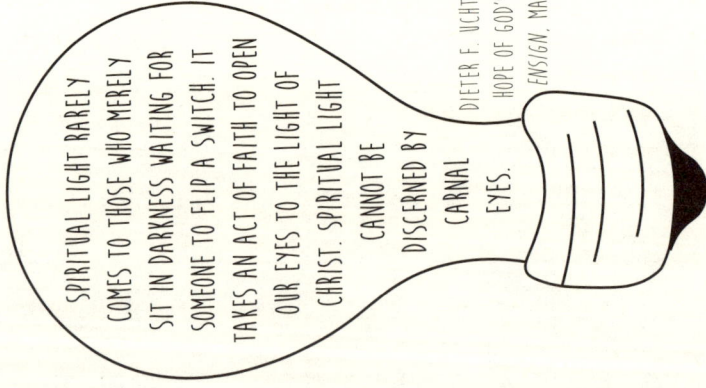

SPIRITUAL LIGHT RARELY
COMES TO THOSE WHO MERELY
SIT IN DARKNESS WAITING FOR
SOMEONE TO FLIP A SWITCH. IT
TAKES AN ACT OF FAITH TO OPEN
OUR EYES TO THE LIGHT OF
CHRIST. SPIRITUAL LIGHT
CANNOT BE
DISCERNED BY
CARNAL
EYES.

DIETER F. UCHTDORF, "THE
HOPE OF GOD'S LIGHT,"
*ENSIGN*, MAY 2013

SPIRITUAL LIGHT RARELY
COMES TO THOSE WHO MERELY
SIT IN DARKNESS WAITING FOR
SOMEONE TO FLIP A SWITCH. IT
TAKES AN ACT OF FAITH TO OPEN
OUR EYES TO THE LIGHT OF
CHRIST. SPIRITUAL LIGHT
CANNOT BE
DISCERNED BY
CARNAL
EYES.

DIETER F. UCHTDORF, "THE
HOPE OF GOD'S LIGHT,"
*ENSIGN*, MAY 2013

# Website Resources

No need to reinvent the wheel, especially when you're using that wheel to drive on the Information Super Highway. The Internet is an endless resource of ideas, recipes, downloads, crafts, lesson materials, music, and instructions for almost anything you'd like to do in your Relief Society Sunday lessons.

Allow me to give you a serious word of caution about doing online searches. If you enter "Women" into a search engine, you will get suggestions for links to all kinds of horrible pornographic websites. You must type in "LDS Women" or "Relief Society," and even then, look at the description of the site before you click on it.

## LDS WEBSITE RESOURCES

- www.lds.org (This is the official website for The Church of Jesus Christ of Latter-day Saints. This should be your first stop on the web.)
- www.jennysmith.net
- www.theideadoor.com
- www.mormons.org
- www.mormonfind.com
- www.lightplanet.com/mormons
- www.ldsteach.org
- www.JeanniGould.com
- www.sugardoodle.net
- www.ldssplash.com
- www.ldstoday.com

## MERCHANDISE

- www.ldscatalog.com (Church distribution center to order materials)

- www.byubookstore.com
- www.ldsliving.com
- www.deseretbook.com
- www.ctr-ring.com

## LDS RELIEF SOCIETY BLOGS

- www.enrichmentideas.blogspot.com
- www.thereliefsocietyblog.blogspot.com
- www.hollyscorner.com/blog/lds-resources/relief-society
- www.segullah.org/daily-special/putting-the-relief-in-relief-society/
- www.feastuponthewordblog.org/category/lessonsrsmp/
- www.happyjellybeans.blogspot.com
- lds.families.com/blog/category/1071

## INTERNET GROUPS

I highly recommend that you join a Yahoo Group. It's free to join and you'll meet some of the nicest people around! People share helpful ideas and tips in a real-time setting. You can receive the emails individually or as a daily digest. Some groups are more active than others so the quantity of emails will vary. Use your resources! There is no reason to do something that another great Relief Society teacher has already done out there somewhere!

- groups.yahoo.com/group/ReliefSociety-L/
- uk.groups.yahoo.com/group/Relief_SocietyLDS/
- groups.yahoo.com/group/ldsreliefsocietypresidency/
- groups.yahoo.com/group/LDSReliefSocietyMeetings/

## CLIP ART

I'm thankful for talented artists who share their wonderful creations with me, since I have trouble drawing decent stick people! Here are the sites of some of those generous artists:

- www.facebook.com/ChristysClipart/
- www.graphicgarden.com/
- www.coloringbookfun.com
- www.oneil.com.au/lds/pictures.html
- www.lds.about.com/library/gallery/clipart/blclipart_gallery_subindex.htm
- www.free-clip-art.net

- www.coloring.ws/coloring.html
- www.apples4theteacher.com
- http://designca.com/lds/

## MUSIC

- www.lds.org/music
- www.mormonchannel.org/radio/music-247www.lds.org /youth/music
- www.defordmusic.com
- www.lds.about.com/library/clipart/blnewera_music_1975 .htm (Great index of all sheet music offered in the *New Era* and *Ensign* magazines from 1975 to 1989.)
- www.ldsmusicworld.com
- www.ldsmusictoday.com
- www.ldsmusicsource.com
- www.ldspianosolo.com
- www.deseretbook.com/LDS-Music/Sheet-Music-Downloads/s /1395
- radio.ldsmusicnow.com

# About the Author

Trina Boice grew up in California and currently lives in Las Vegas where she teaches at the famous Le Cordon Bleu College for Culinary Arts. You can see her yummy food pictures on Instagram! She is also a professor at BYU–Idaho where she teaches in the inspiring Pathway program.

In 2004, she was honored as the California Young Mother of the Year, an award which completely amuses her four sons. She earned two bachelor's degrees from BYU where she competed on the speech and debate team and the ballroom dance team. She was president of the National Honor Society Phi Eta Sigma and served as ASBYU secretary of Student Community Services. She is currently a doctoral candidate at Colorado Technical University—always the eternal student.

Trina also studied at the University of Salamanca in Spain and later returned there to serve an LDS mission in Madrid for a year and a half.

ABOUT THE AUTHOR

She has a real estate license, travel agent license, two master's degrees, and a black belt in Tae Kwon Do, although she's the first one to admit she'd pass out from fright if she were ever really attacked by a bad guy.

She worked as a legislative assistant for a congressman in Washington DC and was given the Points of Light Award and President's Volunteer Service Award for her domestic and international community service. She was selected by KPBS in San Diego to be a political correspondent during a recent presidential election. If she told you what she really did she'd have to kill you.

Trina wrote a column called "The Boice Box" for a newspaper in Georgia, where she lived for fifteen years. She taught Spanish at a private high school and ran an appraisal business with her husband for twenty years. She loves to travel and is a popular speaker in China.

Trina is the author of twenty-one books with another one hitting stores soon. You can read more about her books and upcoming events at www.trinasbooks.com.

Check out her Mormon mom movie reviews at www.MovieReview Maven.blogspot.com and author blog at www.BoiceBox.blogspot.com.

SCAN to visit

www.trinasbooks.com